Gooseberry Patch

A Country Store In Your Mailbox®

Hometown Favorites

A Country Store In Your Mailbox®

Gooseberry Patch
600 London Road
Department BOOK
Delaware, OH 43015
★

1-800·854·6673

How To Subscribe

Would you like to receive
"A Country Store in Your Mailbox"®?
For a 2-year subscription to our 96-page
Gooseberry Patch catalog, simply send $3.00 to:

Gooseberry Patch
600 London Road
Department BOOK
Delaware, OH 43015

Contents

Dedication

To all our friends with
sweet remembrances of penny candy,
county fairs, pancake breakfasts
and ice cream socials!

Appreciation

Thanks to each and every one
of you for sharing your favorite recipes
& hometown memories!

Early Bird Café

Strawberry Popover Pancake

Marla Arbet
Burlington, WI

A wonderful breakfast treat!

2 T. butter
1/2 c. all-purpose flour
1/2 c. milk
2 eggs

1/4 c. mini chocolate chips
1/4 c. sugar
1 pt. strawberries, sliced
Garnish: whipped topping

Place butter in a 9" glass pie plate; place in 200 degree oven until butter is melted. In a medium bowl, beat flour, milk and eggs until well blended. Pour mixture over melted butter; do not stir. Drop chocolate chips evenly over flour mixture. Bake at 400 degrees for 20 to 25 minutes or until edges of pancake are puffed and a deep golden brown. In a small bowl, sprinkle sugar on strawberries and spoon into center of pancake; cut into wedges. Serve with whipped topping. Makes 6 servings.

Pancake breakfasts are a favorite small town tradition!
Held at the local grange hall or church,
look for announcements in your newspaper
for this fun annual event.

Early Bird Café

Lemony Apple Muffins

Vickie

Use different types of apples to change the taste...spicy Fuji or tart Granny Smith are both tasty!

2 c. all-purpose flour
4 t. baking powder
1/8 t. salt
1/2 c. plus 1 T. sugar, divided
1 apple, peeled, cored and
   chopped

1/3 c. butter, melted
zest of one lemon
2 eggs
1 c. milk
1 t. cinnamon

In a large bowl, sift together flour, baking powder, salt and 1/2 cup sugar. Add apple, toss to coat; set aside. In a separate bowl, blend butter, lemon zest, eggs and milk; gently stir into the flour mixture. Divide mixture equally among 12 greased muffin tins. Sift together remaining sugar and cinnamon; sprinkle over muffin tops. Bake at 425 degrees for 15 minutes or until muffins test done in the center. Cool slightly before removing to a wire rack to cool completely. Makes 12 muffins.

A fun way to remember your hometown! Bring out your collection of special ribbons from the county fair or spelling bee, high school pennants, prom invitations and postcards...all are fun additions to your bulletin board and bring back such fond memories.

Sunday Morning Sandwiches

Mary Ann Nemecek
Springfield, IL

For a more colorful variation, add sautéed green and red peppers!

6 hamburger buns
1 stick margarine, divided
1 onion, chopped
4-oz. can sliced mushrooms,
    drained

6 eggs, beaten
Greek seasoning to taste
6 slices American cheese

Lightly coat the cut side of each bun with 1-1/2 teaspoons margarine per side, place on griddle and brown; set aside. Sauté onion and half of the mushrooms in the remaining 2 tablespoons margarine, save remaining mushrooms for another recipe. Stir mushroom and onion together until tender, pour eggs over mixture, then sprinkle Greek seasoning over eggs. As eggs cook, cut mixture into 6 squares with a spatula and turn each to cook on the other side. Place cheese on top of each egg square. To serve, place each egg square on grilled buns. Makes 6 sandwiches.

Mom always wore that fancy hat when we went to church socials!

Early Bird Café

Amish Sweet Rolls

Nikkole Kozlowski
Columbus, OH

There's nothing like homemade sweet rolls warm-from-the-oven!

1/4 c. shortening
2 c. self-rising flour
3/4 c. plus 3 T. milk, divided
1/4 c. butter, melted

1/2 c. sugar
2 t. cinnamon
1 c. powdered sugar
1/4 t. vanilla extract

Cut shortening into flour until mixture resembles coarse crumbs. Stir in 3/4 cup milk; gently blend with a fork. Turn dough out onto a lightly floured surface and knead until smooth. Roll dough out until 1/4-inch thick; brush with butter. Combine sugar and cinnamon, sprinkle evenly over dough. Roll up, jelly roll-style, beginning with the long side. Slice into 1/2-inch thick slices and place on a baking sheet lightly sprayed with non-stick vegetable spray. Bake at 425 degrees for 18 to 20 minutes. Combine powdered sugar, remaining milk and vanilla until smooth; drizzle over warm rolls. Makes 8 to 10 rolls.

"Being raised by my Grandmother has left me with a lifetime of beautiful memories…she was truly a kid at heart! Each day Nanny could be found cooking delicious meals in her kitchen. Offering her southern hospitality, she felt there was always room at the table for one more and was ready at a moment's notice for company."

Tina Smith
Mounds, OK

Bacon & Cheese Waffles

Jennifer Ash
Piffard, NY

For something different at breakfast, try these delicious waffles.

1 egg, beaten
1 c. milk
1 c. sour cream
1 T. butter, melted

2 c. biscuit baking mix
6 to 8 slices bacon, crisply
   cooked and crumbled
1 c. Cheddar cheese, shredded

In a medium bowl, blend together egg, milk, sour cream and butter. Stir in biscuit baking mix; blend well. Mix in bacon and cheese. Pour in enough batter to fill a preheated waffle iron and bake until steaming stops and waffles are crisp and golden. Makes 12 waffles.

Southern Hash Browns

Athena Colegrove
Big Springs, TX

For those who like their hash browns with a little kick!

2 T. olive oil
1 t. paprika
3/4 t. chili powder
1/2 t. salt

1/4 t. cayenne pepper
1/8 t. pepper
6-1/2 c. potatoes, peeled and
   diced

Stir together oil, paprika, chili powder, salt and peppers; set aside. Lightly coat a baking sheet with non-stick vegetable spray and add potatoes in a single layer. Drizzle oil mixture over potatoes and bake at 400 degrees for 30 minutes or until golden brown. Makes 5 servings.

Life isn't a matter of milestones, but of moments.

-Rose Fitzgerald Kennedy

Early Bird Café

Baked Blueberry French Toast

Jena Hollabaugh
Lancaster, CA

This recipe was from a wonderful bed and breakfast where we stayed during our honeymoon. It is now one of our favorite breakfasts!

6 slices sourdough French
   bread, torn
4 eggs
1 c. half-and-half
1 t. vanilla extract
1/2 c. sugar

1 t. cinnamon
1/4 t. allspice
1-1/2 t. cornstarch
2 c. blueberries
1/4 c. butter, melted

Place bread into a jelly roll pan. In a medium bowl, mix eggs, half-and-half and vanilla together, pour over bread, cover and refrigerate overnight. Combine sugar, cinnamon, allspice and cornstarch together, fold in blueberries and place in a greased 13"x9" baking pan. Place chilled bread mixture on top of blueberry mixture, drizzle butter over bread. Bake at 450 degrees for 30 minutes or until golden brown. Makes 2 to 3 servings.

*Before the big parade, invite neighbors over to enjoy
a stack of buttermilk pancakes or waffles hot off the griddle!
Serve fresh fruit, juice and a variety of syrups...blueberry,
honey-maple and strawberry.*

Banana-Almond Coffee Cake

Marlene Darnell
Newport Beach, CA

A morning treat served with freshly-brewed coffee.

1/2 c. butter, melted and divided
2/3 c. brown sugar, packed and
  divided
2/3 c. sliced almonds, divided
2 bananas, mashed
1 egg, beaten

1/4 c. sugar
2 c. biscuit baking mix
1/3 c. milk
1-3/4 t. cinnamon
1/2 t. nutmeg

Pour 1/4 cup of butter into a Bundt® pan that has been coated with non-stick vegetable spray. On top of butter, evenly sprinkle 1/3 cup brown sugar and 1/3 cup almonds. In a mixing bowl, combine bananas, egg and sugar; blend in baking mix and milk. Carefully spoon half of banana mixture into Bundt® pan. Mix remaining brown sugar and almonds, cinnamon and nutmeg; sprinkle over banana mixture. Slowly pour remaining butter over banana mixture, top with reserved half of banana mixture. Use the back of a spoon to smooth out batter. Bake at 400 degrees for 25 minutes or until center tests done. Immediately invert pan onto a serving plate; let sit for 3 to 4 minutes. Remove pan and cool slightly before serving. Makes 12 servings.

"Whenever I went to our little corner market for Mom or a neighbor, I would always earn a dime. This dime was a highly cherished coin, like gold in my pocket because with it, I could get 10 to 20 pieces of candy!"

Sandy Dodson
Indianapolis, IN

Early Bird Café

Cornmeal Pancakes

Linda Hensz
Port Jervis, NY

*My family loves these crispy and delicious pancakes! Serve
with real maple syrup and sausage on the side.*

3/4 c. all-purpose flour
2 T. sugar
1/2 c. cornmeal
4 t. baking powder

3/4 t. salt
5 T. butter
1 c. milk
2 eggs

In a large mixing bowl, blend together flour, sugar, cornmeal, baking
powder and salt. In a small saucepan, melt butter in milk; cool to
lukewarm and add eggs. Add egg mixture to flour mixture; blend well.
Lightly coat a griddle with non-stick vegetable spray and pour 1/4 cup
batter on griddle. Cook for 2 minutes, flip and cook other side for one
additional minute or until pancake is golden. Repeat with remaining
batter. Makes 12 pancakes.

Dressed in our Sunday best.

Baked Apple Pancake

Debbie Beauchamp
Murrells Inlet, SC

*So easy to prepare. While it's baking, the table can be set,
sausage cooked and coffee made...perfect!*

1/4 c. butter
4 to 5 apples, peeled, cored and
   thinly sliced
1/2 c. sugar
1/2 t. cinnamon

6 eggs
1 c. all-purpose flour
1 c. milk
1/2 t. salt
Garnish: maple syrup

In an 8" cast iron skillet, melt butter. Add apples, sugar and cinnamon,
sauté until apples begin to soften. In a mixing bowl, blend together
eggs, flour, milk and salt; pour over apples directly in iron skillet.
Bake, in iron skillet, at 375 degrees for 20 to 30 minutes or until
puffed and pancake tests done in the center. Serve with maple syrup if
desired. Makes 6 servings.

*Spread some maple butter on fresh pancakes or
biscuits. Just combine one stick butter with 3/4 cup
maple syrup and beat until fluffy...yum!*

Early Bird Café

Blueberry-Oatmeal Breakfast Cake

Darlene Hartzler
Marshallville, OH

Substitute fresh raspberries, mulberries or boysenberries to easily invent a new breakfast cake!

1-1/3 c. all-purpose flour
3/4 c. quick-cooking oats,
   uncooked
2 t. baking powder
1/4 t. salt
1 egg

3/4 c. sugar
3/4 c. plus 3 t. milk, divided
1/4 c. oil
1 c. blueberries
1/2 c. powdered sugar
1/2 t. almond extract

Mix together flour, oats, baking powder, salt, egg, sugar, 3/4 cup milk and oil. Fold in blueberries. Spread batter in an 8"x8" baking dish and bake at 400 degrees for 20 to 25 minutes or until tested done. Blend together powdered sugar, almond extract and remaining milk and pour over warm cake. Makes 8 servings.

Glass milk bottles, especially the vintage ones with the cream-top, add a touch of nostalgia to your family's breakfast table! Fill the bottles with a variety of juices or milk and everyone can choose their favorite.

CREAM

Spiced French Toast

Helen Woodard
Necedah, WI

Delicious topped with real butter and pure maple syrup!

3 eggs	1/2 t. pumpkin pie spice
1/4 c. milk	1 t. sugar
1 t. vanilla extract	5 slices bread, thickly sliced

Whisk eggs, milk, vanilla, pumpkin pie spice and sugar; beat well. Coat both sides of bread with egg mixture then cook bread on a hot, well oiled skillet until golden brown. Makes 2 to 3 servings.

"Mrs. Higgins' general store was located near my dad's workshop in Eureka Springs, Arkansas. When I was little, Daddy and I would go to the store and buy a quart of milk and a package of cinnamon rolls to share. I remember the worn wooden floors, the ice box and smiling, white-haired Mrs. Higgins...and sharing ice cold milk with Daddy."

Susan Young
Madison, AL

Early Bird Café

Orange-Cranberry Rolls

Jo Ann

These easy-to-make rolls are so good with a tall, icy glass of milk!

10-oz. tube refrigerated pizza
  crust dough
1/2 c. orange marmalade
2/3 c. dried cranberries

1/2 c. powdered sugar
1-1/2 t. lemon juice
1 t. hot water

Press dough into a 12"x9" rectangle. Spread marmalade onto dough, leaving a 1/2-inch border around the edges. Evenly place cranberries over marmalade, gently pressing into the dough. Beginning with the long side of the dough, roll up jelly roll-style. When completely rolled, pinch the seam to seal but don't seal the ends of the roll. Slice roll in 12 one-inch slices, then place them, cut sides up, in muffin cups lightly coated with non-stick vegetable spray. Bake at 375 degrees for 15 minutes. Remove from muffin cups and place on a wire rack to cool completely. Blend together powdered sugar, lemon juice and water, stir until smooth and drizzle over warm rolls. Makes 12.

Summers by the shore...we'd pack a picnic basket and find the perfect spot to spend the day.

Crispy Waffles

Lisa Silver
Lamoni, IA

*The yeast and egg are the "secret ingredients"
in these waffles!*

1 T. active dry yeast
1 c. lukewarm water
2 T. plus 1/8 t. sugar, divided
1 t. salt

3 c. lukewarm milk
6 c. all-purpose flour
2 eggs, separated and divided
10 T. butter, melted

In a large bowl, dissolve yeast in water with 1/8 teaspoon sugar. In a separate bowl, dissolve remaining sugar and salt in milk; add to yeast mixture. Blend in the flour; beating until smooth. Add egg yolks and combine well. Mix in butter; cover and set in a warm place for about 1-1/2 hours. Stir and add a little more milk if needed to make a smooth batter. Fold in stiffly beaten egg whites. Spoon just enough batter to fill a heated waffle iron and cook until waffles stop steaming and are crisp and golden. Makes 20 to 25 waffles.

There's a lot of charm in our hometowns...why not capture it in pictures? Quirky signs, barns, motels, old houses, storefronts, even picket fences!

Early Bird Café

Flaky Cheese Danish

Jackie Overton
Mattoon, IL

Terrific served on a brunch buffet.

2 8-oz. tubes crescent rolls, divided
1-1/4 c. sugar, divided
1 egg, separated and divided

8-oz. pkg. cream cheese
1 t. vanilla extract
1 t. cinnamon
1/2 c. chopped walnuts

Unroll one package of crescent rolls, separate and place on the bottom of a 13"x9" baking dish; press seams together. Cream together one cup sugar, egg yolk, cream cheese and vanilla. Spread mixture evenly over crescent rolls. Unroll the remaining tube of crescent rolls and place over top of cream cheese mixture. Beat egg white until frothy; brush over crescent rolls. Mix together cinnamon, remaining sugar and walnuts; sprinkle on top. Bake at 350 degrees for 30 minutes. Makes 16 servings.

For a sweet cinnamon flavor, add 2 tablespoons molasses, 1/2 teaspoon cinnamon and 1/4 teaspoon vanilla extract to one cup plain yogurt. Enjoy with fresh fruit or spread on scones!

Cinnamon Pumpkin Pancakes

Paula Johnson
Center City, MN

A great way to enjoy the spicy taste of pumpkin all year 'round.

1 c. all-purpose flour
1 T. sugar
2 t. baking powder
1/2 t. salt
1/2 t. cinnamon

1 c. milk
1/2 c. canned pumpkin
2 eggs, separated and divided
2 T. oil

In a large mixing bowl, combine flour, sugar, baking powder, salt and cinnamon. In a separate bowl, blend together milk, pumpkin, beaten egg yolks and oil. Add pumpkin mixture to flour mixture all at once; stirring until just blended. Beat egg whites until stiff peaks form, then gently fold into pancake batter. Spoon 1/4 cup batter onto a griddle sprayed with non-stick vegetable spray. Cook until bubbles begin to form around the edges, turn and cook until second side is golden. Serve with Apple Cider Syrup. Makes 18 pancakes.

Apple Cider Syrup:

3/4 c. apple cider
1/2 c. brown sugar, packed
1/2 c. corn syrup
2 T. margarine

1/2 t. lemon juice
1/8 t. cinnamon
1/8 t. nutmeg

In a medium saucepan, combine all ingredients. Cook, stirring often, over medium heat until sugar dissolves and mixture is bubbly. Simmer, stirring occasionally, for approximately 20 minutes or until mixture is reduced to one cup. Let stand for 30 minutes to thicken.

Happiness seems made to be shared.

-Jean Racine

Early Bird Café

Old-Fashioned Porridge

*The Governor's Inn
Ludlow, VT*

A few years ago we created this porridge recipe...it's a winner!

3 c. water
1-1/2 t. salt
2 c. long-cooking oats,
   uncooked
2 eggs
1 c. milk
1/4 c. molasses

1/3 c. maple syrup
1/4 c. brown sugar, packed
1/2 t. cinnamon
3/4 t. nutmeg
1/2 T. ginger
1/4 lb. raisins
1/4 c. chopped walnuts

In a saucepan, heat water and salt until boiling. Add oats and cook for 5 minutes; cool. In a large bowl, combine remaining ingredients; add to oats. Pour into a greased 13"x9" pan. Bake, uncovered, at 350 degrees for 2 hours. Serve hot. Makes 4 to 6 servings.

*If you're lucky enough to have an inn or bed & breakfast
in your hometown, treat yourself to a night out!*

Sunrise Granola

Jennifer Hansen
Escanaba, MI

Carry this with you on an early morning hike!

1 c. long-cooking oats,
    uncooked
1/4 c. flaked coconut
2 T. sunflower seeds
1/4 c. wheat germ

1/4 t. cinnamon
2 T. honey
1/4 t. vanilla extract
1 T. oil

In a large mixing bowl, place oats, coconut, sunflower seeds, wheat germ and cinnamon; mix well with fork. In a separate bowl, combine honey, vanilla and oil; blend well. Pour honey mixture into oat mixture; blend well. Spread on a baking sheet and bake at 350 degrees for 20 to 25 minutes, stirring every 5 minutes. Let cool then store in an airtight jar. Makes 1-1/2 cups.

Best friends through school, it was great when we won the tennis tournament our senior year!

Early Bird Café

Golden Doughnut Holes

Lori Collins
Garrettsville, OH

A favorite for little or big kids! We love them with a cup of steaming coffee.

oil plus 1/4 c. oil
2 c. all-purpose flour
1 c. sugar, divided
3 t. baking powder
1/2 t. salt

1 t. nutmeg or cardamom
1/4 c. plus 1 t. cinnamon, divided
3/4 c. milk
1 egg

Add enough oil to a deep fryer to measure 3 to 4 inches, then set at 375 degrees. In a mixing bowl, sift together flour, 1/4 cup sugar, baking powder, salt, nutmeg or cardamom and one teaspoon cinnamon. In a separate bowl, blend remaining 1/4 cup oil, milk and egg together; add to dry ingredients and beat until smooth. Drop 4 or 5 teaspoonfuls of batter into hot oil and cook 3 minutes or until golden. Remove to a paper towel-lined plate while you repeat with the remaining batter. Blend together remaining cinnamon and sugar and while doughnut holes are still warm, roll in cinnamon-sugar mixture. Makes 2 to 3 dozen doughnut holes.

"How well I remember the milkman delivering milk from the dairy to our front door! We'd put the number of bottles we wanted out on the porch and he'd replace them with bottles of fresh milk, the cream still on the top."

Jackie Crough
Salina, KS

Early Riser Special

Susan Henry
Edwardsville, IL

Enjoy all your breakfast favorites rolled into one!

2 8-oz. tubes refrigerated
   crescent rolls
1 lb. ground sausage, browned
1-1/2 c. frozen hash browns,
   thawed
4-oz. pkg. Cheddar cheese,
   shredded

1/4 c. milk
5 eggs
1 t. salt
1 t. pepper
grated Parmesan cheese to taste

Press crescent rolls into a pizza pan to form a crust; spoon sausage over crust. Sprinkle hash browns over sausage, top with Cheddar cheese. In a medium bowl, beat together milk, eggs, salt and pepper; pour over Cheddar cheese. Sprinkle with Parmesan cheese and bake at 375 degrees for 20 minutes, or until eggs are set and cheese is bubbly. Makes 6 to 8 servings.

*We have all got our
"good old days" tucked away
inside our hearts,
and we return to them
in dreams like cats to
favorite armchairs.*

-Brian Carter

Early Bird Café

Country-Style Baked Fruit

Cathy Baugh
Lewisburg, KY

Warm, sweet fruit with a touch of brown sugar...delicious!

15-oz. can apricots, drained
15-oz. can peach slices, drained
15-oz. can pineapple chunks,
   drained

1/2 c. brown sugar, packed
1 stick butter
1 or 2 sleeves round, buttery
   crackers, crushed

In a 13"x9" baking pan, combine apricots, peaches and pineapple; sprinkle on brown sugar. Dot with butter and add cracker crumbs. Bake at 350 degrees for 15 minutes or until bubbly. Makes 8 to 10 servings.

Host a maple sugaring-off gathering for friends and neighbors...it's a great way to get everyone together! Plan a breakfast menu with tasty recipes using maple syrup...pancakes, waffles, biscuits, scones and corn cakes.

Apple Jack Muffins

Zoe Bennett
Columbia, SC

The best combination...apples and cinnamon!

2-1/3 c. all-purpose flour
1 c. plus 3 T. sugar, divided
1 T. baking powder
4 t. cinnamon, divided
1 t. baking soda
1/2 t. salt
1-1/2 c. apples, peeled, cored
   and finely chopped

1 c. buttermilk
1/3 c. milk
1/3 c. ricotta cheese
3 T. oil
1 T. vanilla extract
2 egg whites
1 egg

In a large mixing bowl, sift flour, one cup sugar, baking powder, 2 teaspoons cinnamon, baking soda and salt together. Fold in apples, stir, then make a well in the center of dry mixture. Whisk together buttermilk, milk, cheese, oil, vanilla, egg whites and egg; add to well in flour mixture. Gently stir just until moistened. Coat 18 muffin cups with non-stick vegetable spray and spoon batter equally in each. Combine remaining sugar and cinnamon; sprinkle evenly over batter. Bake muffins at 400 degrees for 18 minutes or until tests done in the center. Makes 1-1/2 dozen muffins.

A basket on your front door filled with mini flags
makes a great hometown welcome!

Early Bird Café

French Vanilla Toast

Sandy Bernards
Valencia, CA

This is a family favorite for breakfast!

3 eggs, beaten
1/2 c. evaporated milk
1/4 c. sugar

1/2 t. cinnamon
1 t. vanilla extract
8 slices bread

Mix eggs, milk, sugar, cinnamon and vanilla together. Dip bread into egg mixture, coating both sides. Toast bread in a well oiled frying pan until golden, turning only once. Makes 4 servings.

Griddlecakes

Cathy Hillier
Salt Lake City, UT

Wonderful served with maple syrup, honey or jam.

1/2 c. milk
2 T. butter, melted
1 egg
1 c. all-purpose flour

2 t. baking powder
2 T. sugar
1/2 t. salt

In a large bowl, beat together milk, butter and egg. In a separate bowl, sift together flour, baking powder, sugar and salt; add to milk mixture. Coat a griddle with non-stick vegetable spray and set to moderate heat. When the griddle is hot, spoon 1/4 cup batter on the griddle and cook until the edges bubble and the underside is golden. Turn and cook the other side. Makes about 16 griddlecakes.

Place some star-shaped floating candles in an enamelware bowl filled with water. They'll cast a pretty glow on your picnic table as the sun sets.

Sausage-Cranberry Quiche

*Wanda Closs
Mt. Airy, MD*

The tartness of cranberries combined with spicy sausage makes a terrific match!

1/2 lb. sage-flavored ground sausage
1/4 c. onion, chopped
3/4 c. dried cranberries
1-1/2 c. Monterey Jack cheese, shredded

9-inch deep dish pie crust, baked
3 eggs, beaten
1-1/2 c. half-and-half

In a large skillet, crumble and cook sausage and onion over medium-high heat until sausage is browned; drain. Remove from heat and stir in cranberries. Sprinkle cheese on bottom of pie crust, then evenly coat with sausage mixture. In medium bowl, combine eggs and half-and-half; whisk until mixed but not frothy. Pour egg mixture over top of sausage mixture in pie crust. Bake at 375 degrees for 40 to 45 minutes or until knife inserted in center comes out clean. Let stand for 10 minutes before serving. Makes 6 servings.

"A wonderful lady named Louise used to sit for me while I was growing up. She taught me many things, like how to tie my shoes and make doughnuts from scratch. Long after I started school and no longer needed a sitter, I still went to visit her and we'd often spend the whole day together."

*Donna Nowicki
Center City, MN*

Early Bird Café

Sugar Plum Bacon

Beth Burgmeier
East Dubuque, IL

Crunchy and sweet...your guests will love it!

1/2 c. brown sugar, packed   1/2 lb. sliced bacon
1 t. cinnamon

Combine brown sugar and cinnamon. Cut each bacon slice in half, crosswise and coat each slice with the brown sugar mixture. Twist bacon slices and place in a 13"x9" baking pan. Bake at 350 degrees for 15 to 20 minutes or until bacon is crisp and sugar is bubbly. Place cooked bacon on foil to cool. Serve at room temperature. Makes 8 servings.

It was a great day when Mom let me pedal my tricycle down the sidewalk to the neighbor's house!

Swiss Oven Omelet

Diane Long
Delaware, OH

*This recipe was handed down to me from my Aunt Nerta.
We think it's perfect for a Sunday brunch!*

8 eggs
1 c. milk
1 t. salt
1/4 t. pepper

2 T. fresh parsley, chopped
8-oz. pkg. Swiss cheese, sliced
   and cut into strips
6 slices bacon, partially cooked

Combine eggs, milk, salt and pepper; beat together and add parsley.
Pour into a lightly oiled 1-1/2 quart casserole dish. Add cheese, top
with bacon. Bake at 350 degrees for 40 minutes. Serve immediately.
Makes 6 servings.

Brown Sugar Baked Oats

Linda Varner
Three Springs, PA

Eat as a breakfast cereal, plain or with milk...or as a yummy snack.

1/2 c. oil
3/4 c. brown sugar, packed
2 eggs
3 c. quick-cooking oats,
   uncooked
1 t. baking powder

1 t. salt
1 c. milk
1 t. vanilla extract
1 T. cinnamon
3/4 c. chopped walnuts

Mix all ingredients together in a 9"x9" pan. Bake at 350 degrees
for 30 minutes. Makes 6 to 8 servings.

*Keep a grade school photo of yourself nearby...for whenever
you want to feel like a kid again!*

Early Bird Café

Grandma's Buttermilk Waffles

Janet Mirku
Oakland, MI

Lost for years, I found this recipe for my Grandmother's waffles when I was going through some old boxes. Growing up, it was always my sister's favorite recipe so I immediately called her!

2 c. all-purpose flour
1 t. baking powder
1 t. salt
1 t. baking soda

2 eggs, beaten
2 c. buttermilk
4 T. butter, melted

Mix together flour, baking powder, salt and baking soda. Add eggs, buttermilk and butter; mix well. Pour batter into a preheated waffle iron and cook until steaming stops and waffles are crisp and golden. Makes 4 servings.

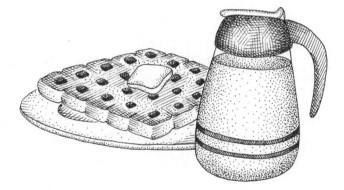

It is threads, hundreds of tiny threads...which sew people together through the years.

-Simone Signoret

Morning Blintzes

Debby Horton
Cincinnati, OH

We serve these at special occasions for family and friends...always a hit!

8-oz. pkg. cream cheese, softened
1 egg yolk
1/4 c. sugar

1 loaf sliced bread, crusts removed
1 stick butter, melted
cinnamon-sugar to taste

Cream together cream cheese, egg yolk and sugar. Roll each bread slice flat and spread with cream cheese mixture; roll up. Dip each blintz into melted butter; roll in cinnamon-sugar mixture. Place blintzes on a baking sheet coated with non-stick vegetable spray. Bake at 350 degrees for 15 minutes. Makes 8 to 10 servings.

"After 4-H judging, my friends and I would roam the fairgrounds. Our favorite rides were the merry-go-round and the tilt-a-whirl! We'd also visit the same vendor every year who made the best taffy. I could stand for hours and watch the taffy pulling machine, then I'd buy a bag and keep it for my very own."

Rebecca Chrisman
Citrus Heights, CA

Early Bird Café

Puffed Pancake

Cheryl Mendelsohn
Deer Park, NY

Serve hot with jam or cinnamon sugar.

6 eggs, beaten
1/4 c. orange juice
1 c. milk
1 c. all-purpose flour

1/4 t. salt
1/2 c. sugar
1/3 stick butter, melted

In a large bowl, combine eggs, juice, milk, flour, salt and sugar; beat well. Place butter into a 13"x9" baking dish, pour egg mixture into dish. Bake at 400 degrees for 20 minutes or until pancake is puffed and golden. Remove from oven, pancake will deflate slightly as it cools. Makes 6 servings.

Still too little for a real pony ride at the fair, my trusty rocking horse did the trick!

Homemade Doughnuts

Heidi Colton
Peachtree City, GA

We've had this recipe for years...it's a real family pleaser!

4 c. milk
1 T. vinegar
4 c. sugar
6 eggs
6 T. shortening
12 c. all-purpose flour

3 t. baking soda
3 t. cream of tartar
1 t. salt
1/8 t. nutmeg
oil

In a small bowl, combine milk and vinegar. In a large bowl, mix milk mixture, sugar, eggs and shortening together; blend well. Add flour, baking soda, cream of tartar, salt and nutmeg; mix well. Cover with towel and let stand for 2 hours. On a generously floured board, roll dough to 1/2-inch thickness and cut with a round doughnut or cookie cutter. Add 4 inches of oil to a heavy pan and using a candy thermometer, bring the oil to 360 degrees. Gently add 3 or 4 doughnuts at a time to the oil, turning them with tongs when one side is golden. Continue to cook until golden on both sides. Remove from oil and let cool on paper towels; repeat with remaining doughnuts. Makes about 7 to 8 dozen doughnuts.

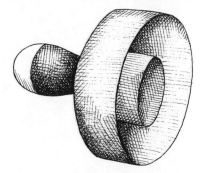

Plant seeds of friendship and tend them with love,
patience and kindness.

-Anonymous

Early Bird Café

Peaches & Cream French Toast

Stephanie Moon
Green Bay, WI

This is absolutely delicious and makes a great breakfast for company!

1 loaf French bread, sliced into
    8 thick slices
3-oz. pkg. cream cheese,
    softened
3 T. peach preserves
1 t. brown sugar, packed

3 eggs
1/2 c. milk
1/2 t. vanilla extract
1/4 t. cinnamon
Garnish: powdered sugar and
    maple syrup

Cut a pocket into each bread slice by cutting from the top crust side, almost to the bottom crust. Be careful not to slice completely through bread. In a small bowl, combine cream cheese, preserves and brown sugar. Spoon about one tablespoon of mixture into each pocket. In another small bowl, beat eggs, milk, vanilla and cinnamon until well combined. Dip stuffed bread slices in egg mixture, letting excess drip off. Spray griddle or skillet with non-stick vegetable spray. Cook bread slices over medium heat until golden brown, turning once, about 2 minutes per side. Lightly garnish each slice with powdered sugar and maple syrup. Makes 4 servings.

If you're hosting a sleep-over, the kids will likely stay up late giggling. Plan to throw a mini breakfast at midnight! Set up a room filled with games, movies and lots of yummy things to eat...bagels, muffins and doughnuts.

Anytime Muffins

Evelyn Pelan
Beavercreek, OH

For a special treat, I sprinkle cinnamon and sugar in the bottom of the muffin pans before filling them.

16-oz. pkg. bran flake cereal
5 c. all-purpose flour
5 t. salt
5 t. baking soda

3 c. sugar
4 eggs, beaten
1 c. oil
4 c. buttermilk

Mix together cereal, flour, salt, baking soda and sugar. Add eggs, oil and buttermilk; stir well. Fill greased muffin cups 2/3 full. Bake at 400 degrees for 15 to 20 minutes. Makes 5 dozen muffins.

Circle skirts, crinolines and convertibles...perfect for an afternoon at the malt shop.

Early Bird Café

Cranberry-Almond Coffee Cake

Kim Martin
Port Republic, MD

The cranberry and almond combination is heavenly!

1/2 c. butter, softened
1 c. sugar
2 eggs
2 c. all-purpose flour
1 t. baking soda
1 t. baking powder
1 t. salt

1 c. sour cream
1-1/2 t. almond extract, divided
16-oz. can whole cranberry
   sauce
1/2 c. slivered almonds
3/4 c. powdered sugar
2 T. warm water

In a large bowl, cream butter and sugar together. Add eggs one at a time, beating well after each; set aside. In a separate bowl, combine flour, baking soda, baking powder and salt; stir into butter mixture alternately with sour cream. Add one teaspoon almond extract. Pour 1/2 of batter into a greased and floured Bundt® pan. Spread cranberry sauce and almonds over batter. Top with remaining batter. Bake at 350 degrees for 50 to 55 minutes. Cool for 5 minutes; remove from pan. Blend together powdered sugar, water and remaining almond extract until smooth; spoon topping over warm coffee cake. Makes 12 servings.

"My favorite hometown memory is of our annual sock hop! We'd look forward to that evening spent under the stars, at Bates Nut Farm. Bales of straw were arranged for seating and the trees sparkled with lights. The band often played past midnight, as we begged for one more dance!"

Vicki Lane
Valley Center, CA

Chocolate Chip-Oat Pancakes

Lynn Nicholl
Gouverneur, NY

These are delicious plain or with warm maple syrup.

1/2 c. all-purpose flour
1/2 c. quick-cooking oats,
    uncooked
3/4 c. milk
1 T. sugar
2 T. oil

1 t. baking powder
1/2 t. baking soda
1/2 t. salt
1 egg
1/2 to 3/4 c. chocolate chips

Beat all ingredients together, except for chocolate chips, until smooth; stir in chips. Measure out 1/4 cup batter per pancake and spoon on a hot, oiled griddle. Cook each side until pancakes are puffy and begin to bubble around the edges. Turn and cook second side until golden. Serves 2 to 3.

Remember when girls used rags to curl their hair? It's still a fun activity for a teenage girls' sleepover! Tear fabric in strips about 8 inches long, then use a spray bottle to dampen the girls' hair. Divide hair into sections, place a fabric strip at the end of each section and roll up. Tie the ends together, leave in overnight and unwind in the morning!

Early Bird Café

Raspberry Streusel Muffins

Carol Jones
Twin Falls, ID

*The aroma of these muffins is a wonderful wake-up
call for your family or overnight guests!*

1-3/4 c. all-purpose flour,
  divided
1/4 c. sugar
1 c. brown sugar, packed and
  divided
2 t. baking powder
1/4 t. salt
2 t. cinnamon, divided
1 egg, beaten

1/2 c. plus 2 T. unsalted butter,
  melted and divided
1/2 c. milk
1-1/4 c. raspberries
2 t. lemon zest, divided
1/2 c. chopped pecans
1 c. powdered sugar
1 T. lemon juice

Sift together 1-1/2 cups flour, sugar, 1/2 cup brown sugar, baking
powder, salt and one teaspoon cinnamon. Mix in egg, 1/2 cup butter
and milk with a wooden spoon. Gently stir in the raspberries and
one teaspoon lemon zest. Grease 12 muffin cups and fill 2/3 full.
Blend together pecans, remaining brown sugar, flour, cinnamon,
lemon zest and butter. Sprinkle the topping over the unbaked batter.
Bake at 350 degrees for 20 to 25 minutes. Mix together powdered
sugar and lemon juice; drizzle over warm
muffins. Makes 12 small muffins.

*Bake a treat for a friend
or neighbor...for no
special occasion.*

Old Time German Potato Pancakes

Wendy Paffenroth
Pine Island, NY

Serve with sour cream or applesauce...yum!

6 potatoes, peeled and grated	1/2 t. salt
1 onion, grated	1/2 t. pepper
2 eggs, beaten	1/8 t. paprika
1/2 c. all-purpose flour	oil

In a large mixing bowl, place potatoes, onion, eggs, flour, salt, pepper and paprika; stir until mixture forms a batter that will drop off a spoon. Heat enough oil in a heavy Dutch oven so that the pancakes will be covered when dropped in. Set paper towels folded onto a tray next to the stove. Working in batches, spoon the batter into the hot oil and fry. Carefully using a slotted spoon, turn pancakes in the oil until both sides are golden brown and then remove quickly to a paper towel-lined tray. Makes 4 to 6 servings.

"When I was a little girl, people would come from miles around to see Main Street decorated for Christmas. There were lights everywhere, bells on each street post and a huge lighted Christmas tree. The streets were bumper to bumper with traffic; everyone was caught up in the magic of the season."

Susie Knupp
Bailey, CO

Early Bird Café

Yummy Hash Browns

Jen Sell
Farmington, MN

My aunt passed this recipe down to me when I first left home and couldn't cook a thing. Because of recipes like this one, I've become a pretty good cook!

8 oz. sour cream
10-3/4 oz. can cream of celery
   soup
2 lb. bag frozen hash browns
1/2 c. pasteurized process
   cheese spread, cubed

1/4 c. margarine, cubed
salt and pepper to taste
1/2 to 1 c. Cheddar cheese,
   shredded

Mix together all ingredients, except Cheddar cheese, in a 13"x9" pan. Sprinkle cheese on top and bake, covered, at 350 degrees for 45 minutes. Uncover baking dish and continue to bake an additional 15 minutes. Makes 8 servings.

Frosty winter days meant ice hockey in the backyard after school.

Sweet Apricot Coffee Cake

Tori Willis
Champaign, IL

I sometimes substitute peaches for apricots, it's just as terrific!

2 c. crispy rice cereal, crushed
3/4 c. plus 3 T. sugar, divided
1/8 t. ginger
1/2 c. margarine, softened and divided
1-1/2 c. all-purpose flour

2 t. baking powder
1/2 t. salt
1 egg
17-oz. can apricot halves, chopped, 1/2 c. syrup reserved

Mix together cereal, 3 tablespoons sugar, ginger and 1/4 cup margarine; blend until crumbly, then set aside for topping. Stir together flour, baking powder and salt; set aside. In small mixing bowl, beat remaining margarine and sugar until well blended; add egg and beat well. Stir in reserved apricot syrup. Add flour mixture, blending well. Spread into an 8"x8" baking pan, then spoon 3/4 cup apricots evenly over batter. Sprinkle with topping and remaining apricots. Bake at 350 degrees for 45 minutes or until cake begins to pull away from the sides of the pan. Makes 9 servings.

The words "Play Ball!" mark the start of baseball season, so why not organize a neighborhood game? Make your own pennant and join in the fun!

Cream of Tomato Soup

Vanessa Dorland
Pocatello, ID

Serve with grilled cheese sandwiches for an old-fashioned favorite!

28-oz. can diced tomatoes,
    undrained
1 c. chicken broth
1/4 c. butter

2 T. sugar
2 T. onion, chopped
1/8 t. baking soda
2 c. whipping cream

In saucepan, mix tomatoes, broth, butter, sugar, onion and baking soda together. Cover and simmer for 30 minutes. Heat cream separately and add to tomato mixture just before serving. Makes 6 to 8 servings.

Beef & Mushroom Soup

Wendy Top
Sunnyside, WA

Add any of your favorite vegetables...potatoes,
cabbage, beans, or corn.

2 cloves garlic, chopped
2 c. onion, chopped
1 c. carrot, sliced
1/2 c. celery, sliced
2 T. butter
1 lb. roast beef, coarsely
    chopped

3 c. beef broth
2 cubes beef bouillon
2 c. water
1/2 c. pearl barley, uncooked
1 lb. mushrooms, sliced

In a large stockpot, sauté garlic, onion, carrot and celery in butter. Add beef, broth, bouillon, water and barley. Boil for 3 minutes. Reduce heat and add mushrooms. Simmer for 2 hours. Makes 8 servings.

Life is playfulness...we need to play so that we can
rediscover the magical world around us.

-Flora Colao

Blue Plate Specials

Ham Salad Sandwiches

Phyllis Peters
Three Rivers, MI

A friend of mine always asked why her ham salad sandwiches didn't taste like mine. I shared this old family recipe, which uses bologna, and she's followed it ever since!

2-lb. ring of bologna
1 onion, halved
6 eggs, hard-boiled and halved
1/2 c. sweet pickle relish

1/2 to 3/4 c. mayonnaise-type
   salad dressing
40 slices bread, buttered

Using a meat grinder, grind bologna, onion and eggs together on a medium setting. Mix relish and salad dressing together; combine with bologna mixture. Spoon mixture equally on 20 bread slices; top each sandwich with a remaining bread slice. Makes 20 sandwiches.

Tuck a tiny American flag toothpick in your sandwich halves! Not only fun, they're great for holding together tall sandwiches like a club or a plump BLT.

Spinach-Tortellini Soup

Cindie Covault
Wilton Manors, FL

Tasty served with warm homemade bread.

2 cloves garlic, crushed
1 T. butter
2 13-oz. cans chicken broth
8-oz. pkg. tortellini
1/8 t. cayenne pepper
1/4 t. pepper

10-oz. pkg. frozen, chopped
  spinach, thawed
16-oz. can stewed, chopped
  tomatoes, undrained
Garnish: grated Parmesan
  cheese

In large saucepan, over medium heat, sauté garlic in butter for 3 to 5 minutes. Add chicken broth and tortellini, heat to boiling. Reduce heat, add peppers and simmer for 10 minutes. Stir in spinach and tomatoes; continue to simmer an additional 5 minutes. Serve topped with Parmesan cheese to taste. Makes 6 to 8 servings.

"When we were kids, summer days full of
blue skies and white fluffy clouds were a
welcome invitation to my sister and me to
lay down in the soft grass and watch the
clouds roll past. We could watch for hours,
and if we got tired of "cloud-naming," we
would simply talk. Those lazy days of
summer made us feel closer somehow."

Linda Haiby
Andover, MN

Blue Plate Specials

Roast Beef Sandwiches

Robin Hill
Rochester, NY

If you'd like, you can substitute crumbled feta for a milder taste.

2 T. mayonnaise
1 T. Dijon mustard
1/4 t. pepper
2 buns, sliced
2 leaves Romaine lettuce

4 slices tomato
4 rings green pepper
4 slices red onion
4 oz. roast beef, thinly sliced
2 T. crumbled blue cheese

Blend together mayonnaise, mustard and pepper; spread on buns.
Layer each sandwich with lettuce, tomato, pepper, onion, roast beef
and blue cheese; add top half of bun. Makes 2 sandwiches.

The fair came to town every
summer...we could've ridden the
rides all day!

Grammie's Chicken-Corn Soup

Sheri Pittz
Feura Bush, NY

*For a tangy taste, add one to 2 tablespoons of apple
cider vinegar to each soup bowl when serving.*

2-lb. chicken
6 qts. water
4 stalks celery, chopped
2 onions, quartered
1 T. fresh parsley, chopped

salt to taste
1/4 t. pepper
3 c. all-purpose flour
3 eggs
2 16-oz. pkgs. frozen corn

In a large stockpot, bring chicken, water, celery, onions, parsley, salt
and pepper to a boil. Reduce heat and simmer for approximately one
hour, or until juices run clear when chicken is pierced. Remove chicken
from stockpot until cool enough to handle. Reserve broth in stockpot;
set aside. In a large bowl, mix together flour and eggs, adding small
amounts of water if dough is too dry. Chop chicken into bite-size
pieces and add to the broth. Bring soup back to a boil and place corn
and 1-1/2 inch pieces of dough into boiling broth. Add more salt
and water if needed. Reduce heat and simmer for an additional
15 minutes. Makes 12 servings.

*Take time to enjoy the simple pleasures of your hometown with
family & friends...cookouts, fireworks, festivals and parades!*

Blue Plate Specials

Tuna-Egg Salad Sandwiches

Kerry Mayer
Dunham Springs, LA

Try this topped with any of your favorite fresh vegetables…cucumber slices, pepper rings or thin slices of celery.

4 eggs, hard-boiled and chopped
6-oz. can chunk tuna in water,
   drained
2 T. red onion, minced
3 T. mayonnaise-type salad
   dressing

2 T. honey mustard
salt and pepper to taste
10 slices bread
5 leaves lettuce
5 slices tomato
1-1/4 c. alfalfa sprouts

Blend together eggs, tuna, onion, salad dressing, mustard, salt and pepper. Divide mixture equally and spread evenly over 5 bread slices. Top each tuna mixture with one lettuce leaf, one tomato slice and 1/4 cup alfalfa sprouts. Top sandwiches with remaining bread slices, slice diagonally if desired. Makes 5 sandwiches.

Enjoy a "girls' day out!" Arrange to meet friends at a favorite café or diner where you can count on the food to be delicious and homemade. Settle in and spend the afternoon together chatting and catching up on each other's families and upcoming plans.

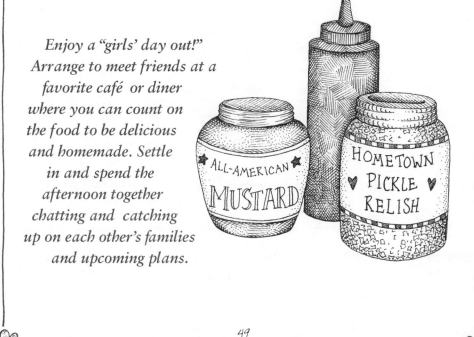

Minestrone Soup

Linda Newkirk
Central Point, OR

My aunt gave this recipe to me about 20 years ago. It's a wonderful main dish soup and it is very easy to prepare.

6 slices bacon
1 onion, chopped
1 c. celery, chopped
2 cloves garlic, minced
2 t. fresh basil, chopped
1/2 t. salt
2 10-3/4 oz. cans bean and
   bacon soup

2 14-1/2 oz. cans beef broth
2 lbs. canned tomatoes
2 c. zucchini, peeled and
   chopped
2 c. cabbage, chopped
1 c. macaroni, uncooked

In a large stockpot, brown bacon, onion, celery and garlic; drain drippings. Add basil, salt, soup, broth, tomatoes, 3 soup cans water, zucchini, cabbage and macaroni. Boil until macaroni is tender. Makes 10 to 12 servings.

*Too much of a good thing
is wonderful!*

-Mae West

Blue Plate Specials

Baked Chicken Sandwiches

Sheila Cottrell
Cincinnati, OH

Make these sandwiches ahead and freeze for those busy nights when you're short on time but you want a hot meal.

4 c. chicken, cooked and diced
10-3/4 oz. can cream of
   mushroom soup
10-3/4 oz. can cream of chicken
   soup
3 T. onion, diced

8-oz. can water chestnuts, thinly
   sliced
1 loaf bread
2 eggs
1 T. milk
6 to 8 c. potato chips, crushed
10-1/2 oz. can chicken gravy

Mix chicken, soups, onion and water chestnuts together. Place mixture on bread slices and top with another slice. Wrap in freezer paper to freeze. When ready to eat, mix together eggs and milk; remove sandwiches from freezer wrap, dip in egg mixture and roll in potato chips. Place frozen sandwiches on a 13"x9" baking dish. Bake at 325 degrees for 45 minutes. Serve with hot chicken gravy poured over sandwiches. Makes 15 servings.

Enjoy an old-fashioned taffy pull! It's a wonderful way to make memories and not hard at all. Find a favorite taffy recipe, then have everyone put on aprons and coat their hands in butter. Roll the taffy in a ball, form teams and start pulling! Repeat until taffy is light and firm, twist and cut into pieces to enjoy.

Best Ham & Cabbage Soup Ever

Kim Johnston-Orazio
Derry, PA

*Just serve this old-fashioned favorite with thick slices of
buttered cornbread and you have a meal!*

4 T. butter
1 onion, chopped
3 potatoes, peeled and cubed
2 carrots, peeled and sliced
2 c. water

13-3/4 oz. can chicken broth
4 c. cabbage, shredded
1/4 lb. cooked ham, chopped
pepper to taste

In saucepan, melt butter and sauté onions until clear. Add potatoes and carrots, stirring occasionally, for 5 minutes. Add water, broth, cabbage, ham and pepper. Cook over medium-low heat for approximately one hour. Makes 4 servings.

Gas for 23 cents!
Now that's a fond memory!

Blue Plate Specials

BLT's

Beth Kramer
Port St. Lucie, FL

Try this updated version of a classic...you'll love it!

1/4 c. mayonnaise-type salad dressing
1 T. fresh parsley, chopped
1 T. green onion, chopped
8 slices bread, toasted

4 leaves lettuce
8 slices pepper bacon, crisply cooked
12 slices tomato
1 avocado, peeled and sliced

In a small bowl, blend together salad dressing, parsley and green onion. Evenly spread on 4 bread slices. Layer each sandwich with lettuce, 2 bacon slices, 3 tomato slices and a slice of avocado; top with remaining bread slices. Makes 4 sandwiches.

"Months before the county fair our kitchen became a busy place filled with jars of home-canned cherry, peach and plum jam and the scent of apple and blueberry custard pies. Mom and my sister would start their quilt; I'd help by cutting out little pieces of calico. Finally the day of the fair arrived and they'd both win blue ribbons...Mom for her quilt and my sister for her apple pie!"

Annette Wesgaites
Hazelton, PA

Corn Chowder

Kathy Grashoff
Ft. Wayne, IN

Spoon this yummy soup into individual bread bowls for a tasty change!

10-oz. pkg. frozen corn
1/2 c. potato, peeled and cubed
1/2 c. onion, chopped
1/3 c. water
1 t. instant chicken bouillon
   granules

1/8 t. white pepper
1-3/4 c. milk, divided
2 T. dry milk powder
2 T. all-purpose flour
Garnish: 1 T. bacon, crisply
   cooked and crumbled

In a large saucepan, combine corn, potato, onion, water, bouillon granules and pepper. Bring to a boil and reduce heat. Cover and simmer about 10 minutes or until potatoes are tender, stirring occasionally. Stir in 1-1/2 cups milk. In a small bowl, stir together dry milk powder and flour. Gradually stir in the remaining milk until smooth. Stir the flour mixture into the corn mixture. Cook and stir until mixture is thick and bubbly. Cook and stir for one minute longer. Sprinkle with bacon pieces before serving. Makes 4 servings.

If you can spend a perfectly useless afternoon in a perfectly useless manner, you have learned how to live.

-Lin Yutang

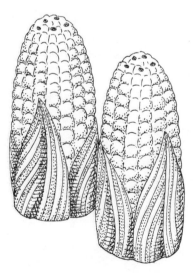

Blue Plate Specials

Deli Skillet Sandwiches

Corrine Lane
Marysville, OH

Serve with chips and pickles for an easy meal!

8 slices rye bread
4 oz. cooked ham, thinly sliced
4 oz. Provolone cheese, thinly
   sliced

4 oz. cooked turkey, thinly sliced
1/2 c. milk
2 eggs

On each of 4 slices of bread, layer ham, cheese and turkey. Top with remaining bread and press lightly to make 4 sandwiches. Cut each sandwich in 1/2 diagonally; set aside. In a 9" pie plate, beat together milk and eggs until well blended. Dip each sandwich into egg mixture, coating both sides. Cook, in a preheated greased skillet, over medium heat until browned, turning once. Transfer to a baking sheet. Bake at 400 degrees for 3 to 5 minutes or until cheese melts and sandwiches are heated through. Makes 4 sandwiches.

A small chalkboard on your front door is nice for friends to jot down a quick message when you're not home. You can easily add 2 screw eyes to the top of the frame, slip a length of wire through and hang on your door!

Asparagus Soup

Tina Stidam
Delaware, OH

Tender, fresh asparagus from the garden is perfect if you have it available. Combined with scallions and potatoes, this soup is really delicious!

2 lbs. fresh asparagus, chopped	1/4 t. seasoned salt
14-1/2 oz. can chicken broth	1/4 t. pepper
4 scallions, chopped	Garnish: sour cream and
2 potatoes, peeled and cubed	tomatoes, chopped

In slow cooker, place asparagus, broth, scallions and potatoes. Cover and cook on low for 6 to 8 hours or until the potatoes are tender. Increase to high heat. Leaving the liquid in slow cooker, remove vegetables and purée in a blender or food processor, in small batches. Add a little of the cooking liquid to the vegetables until mixture is smooth. Return puréed mixture to the slow cooker. Stir in seasoned salt and pepper. Cover and cook on high an additional 30 minutes. Serve garnished with a scoop of sour cream and tomatoes. Makes 4 to 6 servings.

Wow them at the next chili cook-off! Serve your favorite chili recipe with a variety of yummy toppings...sour cream, chives, Cheddar cheese or hot peppers. Use leaf-shaped cookie cutters to cut squares of cornbread into fun shapes for serving alongside your soup.

Blue Plate Specials

Chicken Salad Sandwiches

Susan Smith
London, OH

Served with slices of fresh melon or strawberries, these sandwiches are great for a quick and tasty lunch.

1-1/4 lbs. chicken breast,
   cooked and diced
1 c. celery, thinly sliced
1 c. seedless, red grapes, halved
1/2 c. raisins
1/2 c. plain yogurt
1/4 c. mayonnaise

2 T. shallots, chopped
2 T. fresh tarragon, chopped
1/2 t. salt
1/8 t. white pepper
6 whole-wheat buns, split
lettuce leaves

In a large bowl, combine chicken, celery, grapes and raisins. In a small bowl, blend together yogurt, mayonnaise, shallots, tarragon, salt and pepper. Spoon yogurt mixture over chicken mixture; mix lightly. Divide mixture evenly among buns. Place lettuce leaves over chicken mixture and place tops on buns. Makes 6 servings.

A smile's great. A memory is even better.

-Jacquy Pfeiffer

Creamy Spinach & Carrot Soup

Gail Prather
Bethel, MN

This soup is a great beginning to any meal!

3 T. butter
1 c. onion, chopped
2 T. all-purpose flour
1 c. half-and-half
10-1/2 oz. can chicken broth
1 c. carrots, shredded

10-oz. pkg. frozen, chopped
   spinach, thawed
1/4 t. salt
1/4 t. pepper
1/8 t. nutmeg
Garnish: orange zest

In a 2-quart saucepan, melt butter; add onions. Cook over medium heat, stirring occasionally, until onions are tender. Stir in flour until smooth and bubbly. Mix in half-and-half and broth. Add remaining ingredients. Continue cooking over low heat, stirring occasionally until heated through. Garnish with orange zest if desired. Makes 4 servings.

"*I remember my sister Sandy and I being thrilled when our great aunts took us to the county fair! We were fascinated by the rides, lights, prizes and smell of all the food, but especially the cotton candy...it just melted in our mouths. Before long, our faces and fingers were sticky, my sister even had some in her hair! Our aunts were a little upset over the mess, but we smiled. It was worth it...the cotton candy was so good.*"

Lynette Martin
East Liverpool, OH

Blue Plate Specials

Tomato Sandwiches

Diane Long
Delaware, OH

Use garden tomatoes warm from the summer sun to make these sandwiches extra special.

10 slices pumpernickel bread
3 tomatoes, thickly sliced
10 sprigs watercress
1 red onion, sliced

1 green pepper, sliced
salt and pepper to taste
mayonnaise to taste

On 5 bread slices lay a couple of tomato slices, 2 sprigs of watercress, a slice of onion and a couple slices of green pepper. Sprinkle with salt and pepper. Spread a layer of mayonnaise over remaining bread slices and top sandwiches. Makes 5 sandwiches.

Being ornery on a Friday night before a spin around the town square!

Ham & Cheese Soup

Caroline Kunimura
Richmond, MI

*Searching our pantry for ingredients to make dinner, Mom
created this soup for us. To her surprise, and ours, we
sang her praises...it's wonderful.*

10-3/4 oz. can broccoli cheese
    soup
10-3/4 oz. can Cheddar cheese
    soup
1-1/2 soup cans milk
1 c. pasteurized process cheese
    spread
1/4 lb. cooked ham, cubed

1 onion, diced
1/2 to 1 c. carrots, diced and
    steamed
1/2 to 1 c. celery, diced and
    steamed
salt and pepper to taste
Garnish: fresh parsley and 1/4 c.
    Cheddar cheese, shredded

Mix together soups, milk, 1/2 soup can water and cheese spread. Cook
on medium heat until completely blended and cheese spread is melted.
Add ham, onion, carrots and celery. Let soup simmer for 15 minutes
on low heat, stirring occasionally. When ready to serve, add salt and
pepper, garnish with a sprig of parsley and sprinkle with Cheddar
cheese. Makes 4 to 6 servings.

*Kick back and enjoy a nap under a shady tree!
Spread out a quilt, hang a hammock and
enjoy a frosty glass of lemonade.*

Blue Plate Specials

Barbecue Hamburgers

Sally Bourdlaies
Bay City, MI

A delicious change from grilled hamburgers!

2 lbs. ground round steak
1/2 c. onion, diced
salt and pepper to taste
10-3/4 oz. can chicken gumbo
  soup

1/2 c. catsup
1-1/2 t. Worcestershire sauce
2 T. mustard
8 to 10 hamburger buns

In a frying pan, brown steak and onion; add salt and pepper. Mix in soup, 1/2 soup can water, catsup, Worcestershire sauce and mustard. Let simmer until thick. Spoon over buns. Makes 8 to 10 servings.

Old soda pop bottles make great "vases." Filled with pinwheels and small American flags...they look great lined up along the center of your picnic table!

Cream of Chicken-Rice Soup

Michelle Heurung
Mokena, IL

Prepare this creamy soup and watch it disappear!

4 qts. water
2 boneless, skinless chicken
    breasts
1 onion, chopped
2 carrots, chopped
2 celery stalks, chopped
1/4 c. fresh parsley, minced

1/4 c. butter
2 cloves garlic, minced
1 c. rice, uncooked
salt to taste
2 c. milk
1/2 c. cornstarch

Bring water to boil. Add chicken and cook until tender and juices run clear; reserve broth. Meanwhile, in frying pan, sauté onion, carrots, celery and parsley in butter until tender. Add garlic and cook for one minute. Cut chicken into bite-size pieces. Add sautéed vegetables and chicken to reserved broth. Stir in rice and salt and simmer gently for 15 minutes. Mix together milk and cornstarch; add to soup. Stir until thick. Makes 16 to 20 servings.

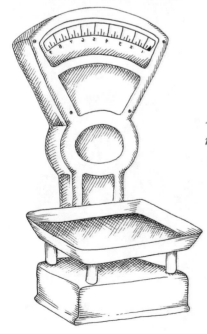

Gather 'round the campfire! A quick phone call invitation to neighbors, and before you know it you'll have a backyard filled with eager kids and parents! Everyone will love an evening spent together under the stars playing flashlight tag, Hide-and-Seek, storytelling and roasting marshmallows.

Blue Plate Specials

Rock Sandwich

Marsha Morlan
Copley, OH

Yes, the name is unique, but it tastes delicious! Use any of your favorites...green olives, black olives, hot peppers or whatever combination you dream up to add a different taste.

2-lb. round pumpernickel bread, unsliced
16-oz. pkg. cream cheese
1-oz. pkg. dry ranch dressing mix

1/4 lb. of 3 types of your favorite lunch meat, sliced
1/4 lb. of 3 types of your favorite cheeses, sliced
1/4 c. olive oil

Partially freeze bread to make it easier to slice. Slice horizontally into about 5 slices, which will include the top rounded piece. Mix the cream cheese with the ranch dressing. Spread part of the cheese mixture on the bottom piece of the bread. Layer, alternately part of the meats, then part of the cheeses. Place the next bread piece on top and spread with part of cream cheese mixture. Layer as previously. Continue this procedure until you get to the top rounded piece. That piece will have the cream cheese mixture on the underside. After all layers of bread are complete, pour olive oil over the top of sandwich, cover with wax paper, place an inverted dinner plate on top and a large heavy rock or 2 bricks on top. Let set overnight in the refrigerator. Take the sandwich out and place on paper towels to absorb the excess oil, slice like a pie. Makes 12 servings.

Vintage lunch boxes are so fun to collect! With lots of colorful designs, they'll look great lined up on a shelf...perfect for corralling clutter, too.

Stuffed Green Pepper Soup

Vicki Hockenberry
Dysart, PA

My family really loves this soup...even the kids!

1-1/2 lbs. ground beef
1 onion, chopped
3 cloves garlic, minced
1 green pepper, chopped

3 14-1/2 oz. cans stewed
   tomatoes, undrained
2 8-oz. cans tomato sauce
6-oz. pkg. white or brown rice,
   cooked

Brown ground beef, onion and garlic together until beef is no longer pink; drain. Add green pepper and tomatoes; cook until pepper is tender. Add tomato sauce and simmer for 15 minutes. Add rice and simmer until ready to serve. Makes 6 servings.

Letter sweaters, argyle socks, flat-top haircuts...and good friends.

Blue Plate Specials

Honey Ham Sandwiches

Carol Lytle
Columbus, OH

Use your favorite style of ham for this sandwich...cajun, maple or smoked would all taste great!

6 slices bread
6 T. cream cheese, softened
6 t. fresh Parmesan cheese, grated

1 onion, thinly sliced
6 slices dill or sweet pickle
9 slices cooked honey ham

Spread 3 bread slices with cream cheese, then sprinkle on Parmesan cheese. Layer on the remaining ingredients in the order listed, top each sandwich with bread slices. Makes 3 sandwiches.

"As soon as summer arrived, so did the lightning bugs...I couldn't wait for night to fall! Daddy would give me a quart jar with holes punched in the lid and partially filled with grass. I'd then spend a couple hours catching lightning bugs. When it was time for bed, I took the jar to my room and as I dozed off, I would watch my magical lantern. Once I was asleep, Daddy would tiptoe in, retrieve the jar and set my glowing friends free."

Susan Young
Madison, AL

Cabbage Soup

Cheryl Kimball
Plymouth, MI

If you'd like, you can place this soup in a slow cooker, set it on low and let it cook for 6 to 8 hours. As it cooks, your home will be filled with a terrific aroma.

1 qt. plus 14-oz. can tomato
   juice
2 cubes chicken bouillon
1 t. onion powder
1 t. Italian seasoning
1 t. garlic powder
1 t. chili powder
1 t. sugar

1-1/2 c. cabbage, chopped
1 c. carrots, chopped
1 c. potatoes, chopped
1/2 c. green pepper, chopped
1 c. cauliflower, chopped
1 c. broccoli, chopped
1 c. zucchini, chopped
1 c. corn

Simmer tomato juice, bouillon, onion powder, Italian seasoning, garlic powder, chili powder, sugar and 1/2 can water for 20 minutes. Add vegetables and bring to a boil. Reduce to simmer for about 2 hours or until potatoes are tender. Makes 6 to 8 servings.

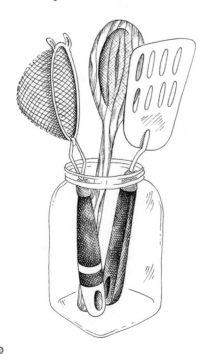

Try something new at your next "girls only" get-together…a fabric swap! We all seem to have a stack of fabric we thought we'd use "someday," but never have, so why not share? You just might find the perfect 1950's checked print you've been looking for!

Blue Plate Specials

French Dip Sandwiches

Denise Collins
Canyon Country, CA

*A favorite family recipe when I was growing up. Mom still prepares
this when my sister and I come home to visit.*

7 to 8 lbs. beef brisket
1/2 t. dry mustard
2 cloves garlic, crushed
1/4 t. onion powder
1/2 t. seasoning salt
1/4 t. cayenne pepper
1/2 t. meat tenderizer
1/4 t. tarragon
1/2 t. cumin

1/4 t. marjoram
1/2 t. seasoned salt flavor
　enhancer
1/2 t. pepper
1/2 bottle of mesquite flavor
　liquid smoke
2 10-1/2 oz. cans beef broth
10 to 15 French rolls, buttered
　and toasted

Arrange brisket on a large piece of aluminum foil and rub with
mustard. Place remaining ingredients, except broth and rolls, over
meat; wrap with aluminum foil. Place in a slow cooker and cook for
8 to 10 hours on low. Remove meat from slow cooker; reserving broth
in slow cooker. Cool brisket and slice. Return meat, with aluminum foil
removed, to slow cooker and add canned beef broth. Reheat until
the meat and liquid are heated through. Serve on French rolls with
a small serving of beef broth on the side for dipping. Makes 10 to
15 sandwiches.

The best things in life are not free,
but priceless.

-Benjamin Lictenberg

Rich Mushroom Soup

Donna Hefty
Salem, OR

This recipe was shared with me by my mother-in-law, Lois.
She doesn't follow a recipe and because our family loves it, I asked
for her help. Together we went through and carefully wrote everything
down step by step.

1 onion, finely chopped
1/2 c. butter
1 lb. mushrooms, diced
1 t. garlic, crushed

1/2 c. all-purpose flour
2 14-1/2 oz. cans chicken broth
1 pt. whipping cream

Sauté onion in butter; add mushrooms and garlic. Sauté approximately
10 minutes, stirring occasionally. Sprinkle flour over mushroom
mixture, stir until well mixed. Slowly add chicken broth. Gently
simmer until thickened. Add cream, heat until very hot, but not
boiling. Makes 4 servings.

Enjoy some old-fashioned fun with
your neighborhood friends!
Set up an area outside for a
game of horseshoes, softball,
tug-of-war, scavenger hunt,
or Red Rover. It's a terrific
way to play together.

Blue Plate Specials

Grilled Summer Burgers

Angeline Haverstock
Portage, IN

Perfect for your Fourth of July barbecue!

1 lb. ground beef
1/2 c. onion, chopped
2 T. green pepper, finely chopped
3 T. catsup
1-1/2 T. prepared horseradish

2 t. mustard
1 t. salt
pepper to taste
4 to 5 hamburger buns

Combine first 8 ingredients. Shape into hamburger patties. Broil in your oven broiler or outside grill for 5 minutes. Turn over and broil the other side until done. Place on buns to serve. Makes 4 to 5 sandwiches.

Barbecued Corned Beef Sandwiches

Roberta Clark
Delaware, OH

Spoon into a wax paper-lined pail and tote to your next family gathering or reunion!

12-oz. jar chili sauce
12-oz. can corned beef,
   shredded

1 T. onion, minced
1 T. green pepper, minced
10 hamburger buns

Cook first 4 ingredients in top of double boiler for 30 minutes. Transfer to a 8"x8" baking dish and bake at 325 degrees for one hour. Serve on buns. Makes 10 sandwiches.

Create a collage to remember special celebrations and
get-togethers! Glue on ticket stubs, postcards,
photos, menus or anything that's a sweet
reminder of that special occasion.

Homestyle Potato Chowder

Wendy Campbell
Provo, UT

Quick to prepare, just fill a thermos for a hearty lunch!

4 slices bacon, diced
1/2 c. onion, chopped
10-3/4 oz. can cream of potato
  soup
1 T. fresh parsley, chopped

1-1/2 c. milk
1 c. cooked ham, diced
15-1/4 oz. can corn, undrained
5 oz. frozen mixed vegetables

In a large stockpot, cook bacon, removing all but one tablespoon of drippings from pan. Sauté onion in drippings. Add remaining ingredients and heat through. Makes 4 servings.

"Grandpa Craig owned a grocery store and I'd spend hours coloring on butcher paper with crayons while we visited. Grandma would often give me a quarter and I'd walk down to the drugstore which had jar after gleaming jar of the best penny candy. After carefully filling my brown paper bag with what I thought was the best selection in the world, I'd go to the playground and enjoy my treasures."

Jeanne Calkins
Midland, MI

Blue Plate Specials

Italian Sausage Sandwiches

Joanne Ciancio
Silver Lake, OH

This is a family favorite...there are never any leftovers.

8 Italian sausages
1 Bermuda onion, chopped
2 green peppers, quartered and
   sliced
1 t. salt
1 t. sugar

1 t. Italian seasoning
2 tomatoes, chopped
8 hoagie rolls
4 t. butter, divided
16-oz. pkg. shredded mozzarella
   cheese, divided

Score the sausages every 1/2-inch; brown in a skillet for 15 minutes or until cooked through; drain on paper towel. Pour off all drippings, reserving 3 tablespoons drippings, and place reserved drippings back into skillet; stir in onion and sauté until soft. Stir in peppers, salt, sugar and Italian seasoning. Cover and cook for 5 minutes. Stir in tomatoes, place sausages on top; cover. Cook, covered, for 5 minutes or until bubbly hot. While cooking, split hoagies, cut out center for boat-shaped shell. Spread equal amounts of butter inside, place on cookie sheet and bake at 350 degrees for 10 minutes. Divide mozzarella cheese equally in the bottom of each hoagie roll; place sausages on top. Makes 8 sandwiches.

First day of high school, bobby socks and all!

Chicken Gumbo

Anne Ogle
Sylacauga, AL

*You'll really enjoy this flavorful soup...great for
warming you up on a chilly day!*

3-1/2 lb. chicken
4 c. water
1/3 c. onion, chopped
16-oz. can tomatoes
1/3 c. rice, uncooked
salt to taste

2-1/2 t. pepper
3 to 4 c. okra, chopped
1-1/2 c. corn
1/4 t. garlic salt
1/2 t. dried basil

Place chicken and water in a Dutch oven. Cover and bring to a boil;
simmer for one hour or until chicken is tender and juices run clear.
Remove chicken from Dutch oven; set aside. When chicken is cool
enough to handle, cut in bite-size pieces and refrigerate until ready
to use. Chill broth for several hours, skim, then return to Dutch
oven. Stir in onion, tomatoes, rice, salt and pepper. Bring to a boil
and simmer for 30 minutes. Add chicken, okra, corn, garlic salt and
basil. Continue to simmer for an additional 30 minutes. Makes 7 to
8 servings.

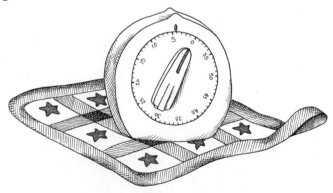

*Get the neighborhood kids together and teach them how
to play some nostalgic games...marbles,
jacks, horseshoes, checkers, pick-up sticks and
hopscotch would all be fun!*

Blue Plate Specials

Club Sandwich

Vickie

Everyone's favorite!

1/2 c. mayonnaise
1-1/2 t. parsley, minced
1 t. green onion, minced
1 t. sweet pickle, minced
2 t. vinegar

3 slices bread, toasted
4 thin slices cooked chicken
3 slices tomato
3 slices bacon, crisply cooked
salt and pepper to taste

Blend together mayonnaise, parsley, green onion, sweet pickle and vinegar until thoroughly combined. Refrigerate until chilled. When ready to prepare sandwich, spread mayonnaise mixture to taste on one side of each slice of toast. Refrigerate remaining spread for additional sandwiches. Layer on chicken, a toasted bread slice, tomato slices and bacon. Season to taste with salt and pepper. Top with last toast slice, cut in quarters diagonally to serve. Makes one sandwich.

Old pickle jars, penny candy jars and glass pantry jars are so collectible! Use them in your kitchen to hold everything from pasta to cookies. They're great in the craft room, too...buttons, bobbins and spools will all be at home in these old-time containers.

Ramblewood Chili

Christina Scharf
New Hartford, NY

For spicy chili fans…this is a great treat!

2 T. butter, melted
1 onion, chopped
1 clove garlic, chopped
1 lb. ground sirloin
1/8 t. salt
1/8 t. pepper
1 red pepper, chopped

14-1/2 oz. can crushed
   tomatoes, undrained
2 15-1/2 oz. cans red kidney
   beans, drained
1-1/4 oz. pkg. chili seasoning
   mix
8 mushrooms, chopped
1/8 t. hot pepper sauce

In a deep skillet, place butter, onion, garlic and sirloin; let sirloin brown. Stirring occasionally, add salt and pepper, cooking on medium heat until meat is completely cooked. Add red pepper, tomatoes, red beans, seasoning mix, mushrooms and hot sauce. Lower heat and let simmer for 20 minutes. Makes 8 to 10 servings.

*Enjoy the little things, for one day you may look back
and realize they were the big things.*

-Robert Brault

Blue Plate Specials

Reuben Sandwiches

Coli Harrington
Delaware, OH

*Melted cheese and tangy sauerkraut combine to make this a
sandwich that's perfect with a bowl of soup or side of coleslaw.*

2 slices corned beef
1 slice Swiss cheese
2 slices pumpernickel bread
1/4 c. sauerkraut

1-1/2 T. Thousand Island salad
   dressing
3 T. butter

Layer one slice corned beef and one slice cheese on a pumpernickel
bread slice. Spoon on sauerkraut and spread on salad dressing. Top
with second slice of bread. Melt butter in a skillet over medium heat,
add sandwich and grill until golden; turn and grill second side. Makes
one sandwich.

*Sometimes the local fire department will
sponsor a community barbecue, but
you can easily plan an at-home version!
Enjoy all your harvest favorites…corn
roasted in the husk, fresh green
beans, crisp salads and,
of course, desserts!
Plan potato sack and
three-legged races,
then after dark, a
big sing-a-long
around a bonfire.*

Creole Soup

Diane Proulx
Woodford, VT

*Simple, but delicious, this soup was always a homemade
favorite from a local cafeteria.*

2 28-oz. cans diced tomatoes
28-oz. can crushed tomatoes
3 10-3/4 oz. cans beef
    consommé soup
2 c. green pepper, diced

2 c. onion, chopped
2 c. celery, chopped
1/4 c. wine vinegar
1 t. prepared horseradish
2 c. macaroni, cooked

Place tomatoes, soup, one soup can of water, green pepper,
onion, celery, vinegar and horseradish in a large stockpot. Simmer
10 minutes; add macaroni and continue to simmer. Makes 10 to
12 servings.

*Search out yard sales or auctions for vintage tablecloths,
dish towels, aprons and pillows with colorful fruit
motifs...they'll add instant nostalgia to your kitchen!*

Blue Plate Specials

Grilled Veggie Sandwich

Wendy Jacobs
Idaho Falls, ID

Use any of your favorite freshly-picked vegetables for this sandwich!

1/4 c. balsamic vinegar
2 T. olive oil
1 T. fresh basil, chopped
2 t. molasses
1-1/2 t. fresh thyme, chopped
1/4 t. salt
1/4 t. pepper
3 zucchini, sliced

1 yellow pepper, coarsely
  chopped
2 red peppers, coarsely chopped
1 onion, sliced
16-oz. loaf French bread
3/4 c. crumbled feta cheese
2 T. mayonnaise
1/4 c. fresh Parmesan cheese,
  grated

Whisk together vinegar, olive oil, basil, molasses, thyme, salt and pepper. Place zucchini, peppers and onion in a plastic zipping bag. Add vinegar mixture; seal and refrigerate for 2 hours, turning bag occasionally. Remove vegetables from bag and set aside, reserve marinade. Slice bread loaf in half horizontally and brush 3 or 4 tablespoons reserved marinade over inside of bread. Lightly coat grill with non-stick vegetable spray, add vegetables and grill for 5 minutes, basting occasionally with remaining marinade. Turn vegetables, baste and grill an additional 2 minutes. Place bread, cut sides down on grill and grill for 3 minutes or until vegetables are tender and bread is toasted. Blend feta cheese and mayonnaise together, spread evenly over cut sides of bread. Layer grilled vegetables on bottom half of bread, add Parmesan cheese and top with remaining bread. Slice into 8 sections. Makes 8 servings.

Remember your favorite teacher? Send him or her a note telling them how much they mean to you. Share favorite memories, let them know what you're up to now and include a photo. Think of how surprised they'll be to hear from you!

Black-Eyed Pea Soup

Kathy Grashoff
Ft. Wayne, IN

*Add bacon, garlic and chilies to a classic soup recipe
and you get this delicious variation!*

6 slices bacon, crisply cooked
   and crumbled, drippings
   reserved
1 onion, finely chopped
1 clove garlic, minced
1 t. salt
1/2 t. pepper

4-oz. can chopped green chilies
4 15-1/2 oz. cans black-eyed
   peas
2 14-1/2 oz. cans beef broth
10-oz. can diced tomatoes and
   green chilies

Blend together onion, garlic, salt, pepper and chilies and add to bacon
drippings; sauté until onion is golden. Add bacon and remaining
ingredients. Increase heat to medium-high and bring to a boil; remove
from heat. Makes 12 to 14 servings.

Ready for the Easter Egg Hunt at
the town square...we couldn't wait
to get there!

Blue Plate Specials

Health-Nut Sandwiches

Mary Scurti
Highland, CA

This is a great sandwich to serve for a luncheon...just pair with a crunchy salad and favorite dessert.

1/2 c. cream cheese, softened
8 slices bread
1/4 c. sunflower seeds

2 boneless, skinless chicken
    breasts, cooked and diced
1 c. alfalfa sprouts

Spread cream cheese on 4 bread slices. Sprinkle on sunflower seeds, layer on chicken and alfalfa sprouts. Top with the remaining pieces of bread; serve. Makes 4 sandwiches.

"Dressed in our finest Easter clothes, girls in ruffled dresses and bonnets and boys in suits, we anticipated finding dozens of colored eggs! "Get ready, set, go!" was called and the hunt began. Laughter, giggles and celebration echoed on the farm and the winners were announced. Afterward, we jumped in the car, huddled together to count our eggs and arrived home joyous."

Phyllis Peters
Three Rivers, MI

Butternut Squash Soup

Pat Woods
Syracuse, NY

*It's hard to believe that this tasty soup can be prepared
so quickly...less than 30 minutes!*

1 T. olive oil
2 cloves garlic, thinly sliced
1 c. onion, chopped
20-oz. pkg. frozen butternut
   squash, thawed and chopped

49-oz. can chicken broth
3/4 c. orzo, uncooked
1/4 c. fresh parsley, chopped
Garnish: fresh Parmesan cheese,
   grated

Heat oil in stockpot; add garlic, onion and squash. Stir to blend and
cook on medium-low for 5 minutes, stirring often. Add chicken broth;
bring to a boil. Reduce heat and simmer until squash is soft, about
10 to 15 minutes. Add orzo and cook until tender, about 6 minutes.
Stir in parsley and serve. Sprinkle individual bowls of soup with
Parmesan cheese. Makes 6 servings.

*The best and most
beautiful things in the
world cannot be seen,
nor touched...but are
felt in the heart.*

-Helen Keller

Blue Plate Specials

Chicken Burgers

Barbara Etzweiler
Millersburg, PA

A yummy twist on traditional hamburgers!

1 lb. ground chicken
1 onion, chopped
1/8 t. garlic powder
1/4 c. fresh bread crumbs
3 T. chicken broth

1 t. Dijon mustard
1 t. salt-free vegetable seasoning
   salt
pepper to taste
4 to 6 hamburger buns

Combine all ingredients, except hamburger buns, in a large mixing bowl. Stir lightly with a fork until well blended. Shape into 4 to 6 burgers. Heat an iron skillet and spray with non-stick vegetable spray. Brown chicken burgers until cooked throughout and nicely browned. Serve on buns. Makes 4 to 6 sandwiches.

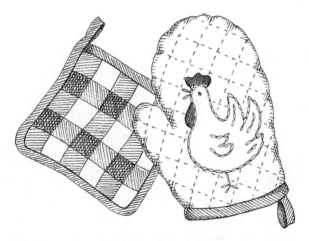

*Plan a recipe swap for your next block party
or family reunion! Ask everyone to share the recipe
for their dish, then slip the copies into a sealable plastic
bag for protection. Each family can go home with new favorites.*

Cream of Spinach Soup

Cathy Adamiec
Kailua, HI

Warm and filling, this creamy soup is all you need for lunch or dinner.

10-oz. pkg. frozen, chopped
   spinach
2 c. water
1 onion, chopped
2 T. butter
2 cubes beef bouillon

1/2 c. orzo, uncooked
10-3/4 oz. can cream of
   mushroom soup
1 c. sour cream
1 T. lemon juice

Place spinach in saucepan with water. Bring to a boil, breaking up spinach. Reduce to simmer, making sure spinach is no longer frozen. Sauté onion in butter. Add bouillon, onion and orzo to spinach mixture; simmer for 20 minutes. In separate bowl, combine cream of mushroom soup and sour cream. Add to spinach mixture and stir until well blended. Add lemon juice; mix well. Continue to simmer for a couple of minutes. Serves 4 to 6.

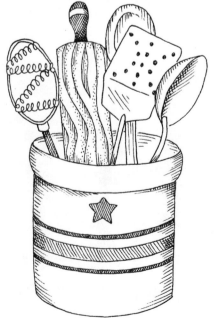

Let the kids discover, and grandparents remember, the joys of penny candy! Fill antique apothecary or canning jars with a variety of candies...gumdrops, licorice, caramels, sour balls, root beer barrels, peppermints and lemon drops. Sit several filled jars on cupboard shelves and let everyone choose their favorites!

Blue Plate Specials

All-American Pitas

Donna Nowicki
Center City, MN

Fill your pita with a variety of your favorite veggies and cheese,
you'll have a light and healthy lunch!

8-oz. pkg. sliced bologna, cut
    into thin strips
3 c. cabbage, shredded
2 T. green pepper, chopped
2 T. onion, chopped
1 carrot, shredded

2/3 c. mayonnaise
3 T. prepared horseradish
1 tomato, coarsely chopped
6 slices American cheese, cut in
    half diagonally
6 6-inch pita pockets, halved

In a large bowl, combine first 7 ingredients; mix well. Refrigerate at
least one hour. Before serving, stir in tomato. To assemble, insert
cheese slice and spoon about 1/3 cup filling into each pita pocket half.
Makes 6 servings.

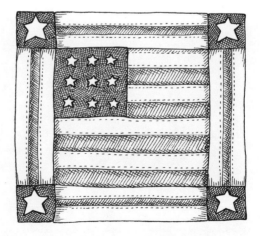

The moon belongs to ev'ryone, the best things in life are free,
the stars belong to ev'ryone, they gleam there for you and me.

-Buddy Desylva

Baked Tuna Sandwiches

Rosalie Benson
Coats, NC

A friend shared this recipe with me and, after 40 years, these still remain our family's favorite sandwich.

2 6-oz. cans tuna packed in
    water, drained
3 to 4 stalks celery, chopped
1 bunch green onion, chopped

3 carrots, grated
3/4 c. Cheddar cheese, grated
mayonnaise to taste
1 loaf sourdough bread, sliced

Mix together tuna, celery, onion, carrots and cheese; add just enough mayonnaise to hold mixture together. Spread mixture on bread slice and cover with a second slice. Place each sandwich in a wax paper sandwich bag. Fold over the top of the bag and place sandwiches in a single layer on a cookie sheet. Bake at 350 degrees for 15 minutes or until bread toasts and cheese melts. Makes 6 servings.

Remember biking down the block to your best friend's house for a day of play?

Blue Plate Specials

Mulligatawny Soup

Robin Guyor
Berkley, MI

This is one of my favorite fall recipes...enjoy!

1 to 1-1/2 lb. chicken breast, cooked and chopped
4 c. chicken broth
1 onion, sliced
1 carrot, sliced
1 stalk celery, sliced
2 T. butter
2 onions, finely chopped

2 Granny Smith apples, peeled, cored and sliced
3 T. all-purpose flour
1 T. curry powder
1 bay leaf
1/4 t. allspice
5 T. light cream

Place chicken in a heavy saucepan. Add broth, onion, carrot and celery; simmer, covered, for one hour. Melt butter in a separate saucepan and sauté onions and apples together for 3 minutes. Stir in flour and curry powder, continue to cook for one minute. Add butter mixture to the soup, along with the bay leaf and allspice. Cover and simmer an additional 15 minutes; stir in cream. Continue cooking for 5 minutes or until chicken is heated throughout. Remove bay leaf before serving. Makes 8 servings.

"For the 4th of July parade, my brothers, sisters and I would spend days "dressing-up" our bikes! Crêpe paper and balloons made us look and feel special as we peddled down Main Street. Baseball cards were placed in our bicycle spokes so we could sound special, too! I can still hear the "clickity-clack" of all those bikes and baseball cards."

Richard Welsch
Gooseberry Patch

Quarterback Soup

Trey Lee
Pensacola, FL

Perfect for a tailgate party! Serve with a 6-foot sub,
veggie tray and frosty sodas.

2 to 3 lbs. ground beef
1 to 2 onions, chopped
1 clove garlic, minced
2 T. butter
2 15-oz. cans beef broth
2 10-oz. cans diced tomatoes
   with green chilies
1 c. potatoes, diced

1 c. carrots, diced
1 c. celery, diced
14-1/2 oz. can French-style
   green beans
1 c. red wine
1 T. fresh parsley, minced
1/2 t. dried basil
salt and pepper to taste

In a large frying pan, brown ground beef and crumble into small pieces. Drain drippings and discard. In a large soup pot, sauté onions and garlic in butter until the onions are tender. Add ground beef and remaining ingredients to the soup pot; stir well. Bring the pot to a boil, then reduce heat. Simmer the soup until vegetables are tender, about 30 to 40 minutes. Serves 6 to 8.

Search tag and yard sales
for vintage kitchen tins that
were once filled with spices,
baking soda, coffee, or tea.
They bring a nostalgic feel to
your kitchen sitting on an
old cupboard or dry sink.

Slow-Cooked Pepper Steak

Dianne Mahan
Pilot Mound, IA

Serve over noodles or rice for a filling homestyle dinner.

1-1/2 to 2-lbs. round steak
2 T. oil
1/4 c. soy sauce
1 c. onion, chopped
1 clove garlic
1 t. sugar
1/2 t. salt

1/4 t. pepper
1/4 t. ginger
16-oz. can chopped tomatoes,
   undrained
2 green peppers, sliced
1/2 c. cold water
1 T. cornstarch

Cut beef into 3"x1" strips, brown in oil in skillet. Transfer to a slow cooker. Combine next 7 ingredients and pour over beef. Cover and cook on low for 5 to 6 hours or until meat is tender. Add tomatoes and green peppers, cook on low for one hour longer. Combine water and cornstarch to make a paste. Stir liquid into slow cooker and cook on high until thick. Makes 6 to 8 servings.

You can easily bring nostalgia to your kitchen! Search your local flea market and yard sales for colorful salt and pepper shakers, juicers, utensils with brightly colored handles, tin picnic baskets and bread boxes.

Hometown Diner

Country Pork Chops & Gravy

Dawn Smith
Cape Girardreau, MO

This meal is so quick and easy to make. I can always count on it to turn out tender and full of great flavor!

salt and pepper to taste
4 pork chops
3/4 c. all-purpose flour
3 T. oil

10-3/4 oz. can cream of
  mushroom soup
1 soup can milk

Salt and pepper pork chops then coat with flour. Brown chops in oil over medium heat. In a 13"x9" casserole dish, mix remaining ingredients; place chops in gravy mixture. Bake at 325 degrees for 20 minutes. Makes 4 servings.

Black-Eyed Pea Skillet Dinner

Lesley Litrenlo
Ft. Lauderdale, FL

You'll love this with slices of warm, crusty bread!

1 lb. ground beef
1 sweet onion, coarsely chopped
1 green pepper, coarsely chopped
2 15-1/2 oz. cans black-eyed
    peas, drained

2 14-1/2 oz. cans whole
    tomatoes, coarsely chopped
    and undrained
salt and pepper to taste

In skillet, brown beef and onion. Add remaining ingredients and simmer for 20 minutes. Makes 4 servings.

One joy scatters a hundred gifts.

-Chinese Proverb

Hearty Beefy Pie

Shari Spackman
Manitowoc, WI

This recipe satisfies my meat and potatoes husband,
plus gives him a little bit of vegetables, too!

1 lb. ground beef
1 onion, diced
10-3/4 oz. can vegetable and
   barley soup
10-3/4 oz. can golden
   mushroom soup

3 potatoes, peeled and diced
4 carrots, diced
salt and pepper to taste
2 9-inch pie crusts, unbaked

Brown ground beef and onion until beef is no longer pink and onions are transparent; drain. Add soups, potatoes and carrots; mix well. Salt and pepper to taste. Divide mixture in half and place into two 9" pie pans. Cover each with a pie crust, crimp edges and cut slits to vent. Bake at 350 degrees for 50 minutes. Makes 16 servings.

The "picture pony" came
to our neighborhood
every year.

Hometown Diner

Old-Fashioned Spaghetti Bake

Margie Schaffner
Altoona, IA

*When my children come home to visit, this
is their number one request!*

2 lbs. ground beef
1 onion, chopped
1 green pepper, chopped
1 lb. spaghetti, broken and
   cooked

14-3/4 oz. cream-style corn
15-oz. can plus 10-3/4 oz. can
   tomato soup
3.8-oz. can sliced, black olives
3 c. Cheddar cheese, shredded

In a skillet, brown ground beef and sauté onion and pepper. In a
2-quart oven-proof bowl, mix together ground beef mixture and
remaining ingredients; cover. Bake at 300 degrees for 1-1/2 hours.
Makes 10 to 12 servings.

*"Each year our hometown hosted an annual
Memorial Day celebration and I always
rode my horse in the parade. He was pretty
spirited and usually danced down Main
Street to whatever music the band marching
ahead of us was playing. The best part of
being in the parade though, was receiving a
participants' ticket which entitled me to free
ice cream...what a special treat!"*

Corky Hines
Walworth, NY

Baked Chicken

Teresa Deal
Gooseberry Patch

When I ask my children what their favorite dinner is, they always reply, "That good chicken with the creamy, crunchy sauce!" I'm always happy to grant their request because this recipe is so quick and easy to prepare.

4 boneless, skinless chicken
　breasts
4 slices Swiss cheese
10-3/4 oz. can cream of chicken
　soup

1/4 c. milk
1 c. stuffing mix
1/2 stick butter, melted

Place chicken in a buttered 9"x9" baking dish. Top each chicken piece with a slice of cheese. Mix soup and milk together; pour over chicken. Sprinkle stuffing mix over soup and drizzle with butter. Bake, uncovered, at 350 degrees for 50 to 55 minutes. Makes 4 servings.

Have some hometown fun...turn your dining room into a soda shoppe! Group round tables with vintage-style chairs, then top each table with a checkered table cloth. Give your "customers" whimsical menus featuring dinner specials that include burgers, fries, shakes, malts and sundaes!

Hometown Diner

Alabama-Style Pork Tenderloin

Debra Donaldson
Florala, AL

My husband brought home pork tenderloins and I couldn't find a recipe I really liked, so I created this one!

3 c. orange juice	1-1/2 to 2-lb. pork tenderloin
1/4 c. soy sauce	2 T. oil
2 T. garlic, chopped	1 T. all-purpose flour
2 T. dried rosemary	1 onion, sliced
3 oz. frozen lemonade	1 green pepper, sliced

Combine orange juice, soy sauce, garlic, rosemary and lemonade together; divide in half. Place half of the marinade into the refrigerator and place the remaining half into a plastic zipping bag. Slice the tenderloin into one-inch pieces. Place the tenderloin in the plastic bag with marinade, turn bag several times to make sure tenderloin is coated with marinade. Keep meat and marinade in zipping bag, and refrigerate for several hours or overnight. Heat oil in a skillet and place marinated tenderloin in skillet; discard marinade in the plastic zipping bag. Brown the tenderloin pieces on both sides. Remove from skillet and let drain on paper towel. Place flour, onion, pepper and tenderloin into a plastic cooking bag; shake thoroughly. Arrange tenderloin mixture in a 13"x9" baking dish; set aside. Remove reserved marinade from refrigerator and pour over the tenderloin mixture. Bake at 350 degrees for 30 to 40 minutes. Makes 4 servings.

Of all of nature's gifts to the human race,
what is sweeter to a man
than his children?

-Cicero

Mom's Manicotti

Bobbi Carney
Aurora, CO

Very simple...very tasty!

1/2 lb. ground beef
1 clove garlic, pressed
1 c. cottage cheese
8 oz. mozzarella cheese,
    shredded and divided

1/2 t. salt
1/2 c. mayonnaise
8 manicotti, cooked
16-oz. jar spaghetti sauce
1/2 t. dried oregano

Brown beef and garlic; drain fat. Mix cottage cheese, half of mozzarella cheese, salt and mayonnaise together; stir in beef mixture. Fill each manicotti with about 1/4 cup meat filling. Place in an ungreased 13"x9" baking dish; cover with spaghetti sauce. Sprinkle with oregano and remaining mozzarella; cover with aluminum foil. Bake at 350 degrees for 15 minutes. Remove aluminum foil; bake an additional 10 minutes. Makes 4 to 6 servings.

"My sister and I used to run down to the store for a bottle of soda pop when we were young. The store was on the first floor of a small house and the owners lived upstairs. One day my sister and I set our bottles of pop on the counter to pay and shock set in as we were told that it was no longer 5 cents, but 10 cents a bottle! What a letdown!"

Susan Brzozowski
Ellicott City, MD

Saucy Slow Cooker Beef

Helen Polson
Beattie, KS

Great to come home to...or take to a company potluck!

2 to 3-lb. round steak, coarsely
    chopped
1 onion, chopped
1 green pepper, sliced
2 c. carrots, chopped
1 zucchini, thinly sliced

1-1/2-oz. pkg. dry spaghetti
    sauce mix
15-oz. can chopped tomatoes,
    undrained
8-oz. can tomato sauce

Place meat in slow cooker and add remaining ingredients in
order listed. Cook on low for 8 hours or high for 5 to 6 hours.
Makes 6 to 8 servings.

We loved playing on that slide in our backyard!

Red Pepper & Sausage Loaf

Barb Bargdill
Gooseberry Patch

Easy for a family picnic...just slice, wrap in
aluminum foil and pack in your basket.

6 mild Italian sausages
1/4 c. butter
1 clove garlic, minced
1 lb. loaf Italian bread, cut in
   half horizontally

2 red peppers, cut lengthwise
   into wide strips
6 oz. mozzarella cheese, sliced
mustard to taste

Prick sausages in several places, then place in a frying pan; add enough water to cover. Bring to a boil over high heat, reduce heat to low, cover and simmer an additional 5 minutes. Drain sausages and set aside. Melt butter in a small pan over medium heat; stir in garlic. Brush garlic butter evenly over cut sides of each bread half; set aside. On 12-inch long metal skewer, thread whole sausages and pepper horizontally, running skewer through the center of each. Place on a lightly greased grill 4 to 6 inches above hot coals. Cook, turning occasionally, until sausages are well browned on the outside and hot throughout. Set bread halves, cut side down, on grill. Cook until bread is slightly browned, about one to 2 minutes. Overlap cheese slices on one bread half. Top with sausage and pepper skewer; set top of bread in place and pull out skewer. Cut into 6 portions; add mustard. Makes 6 servings.

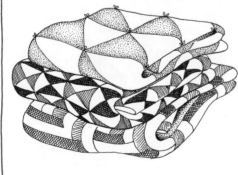

Ask friends that are dear to you
if they can stitch a quilt square to
contribute to a friendship quilt.
Then, on a chilly day, invite
everyone over for homemade
cocoa and fresh-from-the-oven
cookies. With all their help, by the
time the cookies are gone, you'll
have a keepsake quilt to treasure.

Hometown Diner

Cabbage Rolls

Mary Feireich
Dublin, OH

This has always been my favorite dish.

1 head cabbage
1 lb. ground beef, browned
1 onion, chopped
1-1/2 c. rice, uncooked
1 green pepper, diced

salt and pepper to taste
2   10-3/4 oz. cans tomato soup,
    divided
tomato juice, optional

Cut a circle around the core of the cabbage to loosen the leaves, drop them into a pot of boiling, salted water. Let boil for 3 to 4 minutes. Select 8 of the larger outer leaves. Lay them flat and cut out a small "V" shape from the root end to remove the hard spine. Mix ground beef, onion, rice, green pepper, salt, pepper and one can tomato soup together. Fill each leaf and roll tightly. Line a glass 13"x9" baking dish with unused leaves. Place cabbage rolls seam side down in dish. Pour remaining tomato soup over top. Bake at 350 degrees for 3 hours. Keep moist by adding tomato juice, if necessary. Makes 4 servings.

Hats off!
Along the street here comes
a blare of bugles, a ruffle of drums,
a flash of colors beneath the sky;
Hats off!
The flag is passing by.

-Henry Bennett

Ginger & Peach Chicken

John Sgambellone
Delaware, OH

My grandmother used to make this for Sunday dinner...try using fresh peaches for an even better flavor!

4 boneless, skinless chicken breasts
8-oz. can sliced peaches, juice reserved
1 t. cornstarch
1/2 t. ginger

1/4 t. salt
4 oz. sliced water chestnuts, drained
2 c. rice, cooked
6-oz. pkg. frozen pea pods, cooked and drained

Spray a large skillet with non-stick vegetable spray. Preheat skillet over medium-high heat and add chicken; cook for 8 to 10 minutes or until tender and juices run clear, turning to brown evenly. Remove chicken from skillet and set aside. In a measuring cup, add enough water to reserved peach juice to equal 1/2 cup. Stir in cornstarch, ginger and salt. Add to skillet, cook and stir until thick and bubbly. Cook and stir for one additional minute. Gently mix in peaches and water chestnuts; heat through. On individual plates arrange rice, pea pods and chicken. Spoon sauce over chicken and serve. Makes 4 servings.

"What I remember most about growing up in our quiet town were the warm summer evenings. As kids, we'd would gather under a street light with our ice cream money in hand. Patiently, we'd wait for the ringing of the bells from the ice cream truck. After having our treat, we'd play games until our mothers called us in."

Barbara Tuve
Montvale, NJ

Cheesy Swiss Pie

Roxanne Bixby
West Franklin, NH

Really delicious! Simply cut in wedges and serve with fresh fruit.

1/3 lb. ground beef
1 onion, chopped
2 to 3 T. green peppers, chopped
9-inch pie crust, unbaked
6 slices Swiss cheese, divided

salt and pepper to taste
10-oz. pkg. frozen, chopped
  spinach, cooked
1 egg, beaten

Brown ground beef, onion and green peppers. Drain and spread into the bottom of pie crust. Arrange half of cheese over meat. Season lightly with salt and pepper. Mix spinach with egg, spoon evenly over cheese. Bake at 450 degrees for 10 minutes, then reduce heat to 325 degrees and bake an additional 20 minutes. During the last 5 minutes, place the remaining cheese on top and return to oven to melt. Makes 6 to 8 servings.

An ice cream cone from the general store was my favorite treat!

Sweet & Sour Pork

Barb Eickhoff
Fountain, MN

A dish you can always count on to satisfy hungry appetites!

2/3 c. brown sugar, packed
2 T. cornstarch
2 t. dry mustard
1/2 c. catsup
1/2 c. water
15-oz. can pineapple chunks,
   undrained

2 T. soy sauce
salt and pepper to taste
3 lbs. pork, cubed and browned
1 onion, chopped
1 green pepper, chopped
6 to 8 c. white rice, cooked

Combine brown sugar, cornstarch, mustard, catsup, water, pineapple, soy sauce, salt and pepper until thick and smooth. Place pork in a 2-quart baking dish; pour brown sugar mixture over pork. Bake at 350 degrees for 1-1/2 hours. When 10 minutes are remaining in baking time, add onion and green pepper to baking dish. To serve, spoon over rice. Makes 4 to 6 servings.

If you want to feel rich
just count all of the
things you have that
money can't buy.

-Anonymous

Hometown Diner

Melt-in-Your-Mouth Sausages

Gloria Kaufmann
Orrville, OH

*This is a family favorite, because it tastes great, is easy to prepare
and makes a large amount...great for company!*

8 Italian sausages
48-oz. can spaghetti sauce
6-oz. can tomato paste
1 green pepper, chopped
1 onion, thinly sliced
1 T. grated Parmesan cheese

1 t. dried parsley
1 c. water
1 lb. spaghetti, cooked
Garnish: grated Parmesan
   cheese

Place sausage in skillet; cover with water. Simmer for 10 minutes;
drain and slice. Meanwhile, place next 7 ingredients in slow cooker;
add sausage. Cover and cook on low for 4 hours. Increase temperature
to high; cook for one additional hour. Serve over spaghetti. Sprinkle
with Parmesan cheese before serving. Makes 8 servings.

*Old pop bottle carriers are great for toting seed packets
and small garden tools, squares of fabric and spools
of thread, picnic items, or even bottles of pop!*

Shepherd's Pie

Ann Simko
Bloomsburg, PA

*Not really a pie, but tender vegetables and beef hidden
under a layer of golden mashed potatoes.*

1 green pepper, sliced
1 yellow pepper, sliced
1 red pepper, sliced
1 onion, sliced
2 lbs. ground beef, browned
28-oz. can whole tomatoes,
   drained and coarsely
   chopped
cayenne pepper to taste

hot pepper sauce to taste
1 t. dried thyme
1 t. dried rosemary
1 t. dried basil
salt and pepper to taste
cornstarch or all-purpose flour,
   optional
6 to 8 potatoes, peeled, cooked
   and mashed

In a large skillet, add peppers and onion to ground beef. Mix in tomatoes and seasonings. If needed, add cornstarch or flour to thicken; let simmer. Pour beef mixture into a 13"x9" baking dish, top with mashed potatoes. Bake at 350 degrees for approximately 30 minutes. Makes 6 servings.

"Nothing could ever compete with the excitement of the yearly visit of the carnival for summer fun! Like most kids, I would wait in line with great anticipation, then, approaching the ticket booth, I'd lay down my quarters and pick up my ticket. As the carousel stopped, I'd wander around looking for the perfect horse. Finding him, I'd climb aboard, and imagine I was riding off on some grand adventure."

Janice Leffew
Seattle, WA

Creamed Chicken

Susan Por
Massillon, OH

This recipe was handed down from my mother. Served over mashed potatoes and biscuits, I think it's the best ever!

4 boneless, skinless chicken
    breasts
1 stick butter
10 T. all-purpose flour

3-1/2 c. milk
4 to 6 cubes chicken bouillon
pepper to taste

In a stockpot, place chicken and enough water to cover; simmer until juices run clear when chicken is pierced, about 20 minutes. Remove chicken from stockpot, reserving 3-1/2 cups broth. Set chicken aside until cool, then chop into bite-size pieces. In a saucepan, melt butter and slowly add flour, stirring constantly. Gradually add reserved broth; continue stirring. Pour milk into mixture, add bouillon and chicken; pepper to taste. Makes 4 servings.

Always a friendly face at
our local diner.

Homestyle Stuffed Peppers

Linda Telo
Powell, TN

Serve with a salad and hot bread...mmm!

1 T. onion, chopped
2 T. butter
1 lb. ground beef, browned
1/2 c. instant rice, cooked
8-oz. can stewed tomatoes

1 t. salt
1/4 t. pepper
1 T. fresh parsley, chopped
3 peppers, halved horizontally
8-oz. can tomato sauce

Sauté onion in butter. In a bowl, mix together ground beef, rice, onion, tomatoes, salt, pepper and parsley. Arrange peppers in an 8"x8" baking dish. Fill peppers with ground beef mixture. Mix tomato sauce with one can water and pour over peppers. Cover dish with aluminum foil. Bake, covered, at 350 degrees for one hour. Makes 3 to 4 servings.

Heading out to a big community event...homecoming, auction, school concert or football game? Save time for all the fun by having a buffet supper right in the kitchen, it's simple and easy because everything can be made the day before! Serve chili with toppings, 24-hour salad, corn bread and icy milk.

Hometown Diner

Grandmother's Beef Stroganoff

Holly Davis
High Point, NC

This is my grandmother's recipe. Everytime I eat it,
it makes me feel like a little girl again!

1 lb. ground beef
1/2 c. onion, sliced
2 T. butter
10-3/4 oz. can golden
    mushroom soup

1/2 c. sour cream
1/3 c. water
1-1/2 c. rice, cooked

Brown ground beef and onion in butter; drain. Add soup, sour cream
and water. Simmer until heated through and serve over rice. Makes
6 servings.

Chuck Wagon Salisbury Steak

Donna Zink
Lapeer, MI

Good, old-fashioned cooking! Serve with mashed potatoes, homemade
rolls and garden-fresh green beans for a hearty meal.

2 c. corn flake cereal, crushed
1 egg
1/2 c. barbecue sauce

1-1/2 t. salt
1/4 t. pepper
1 lb. ground beef

In a mixing bowl, combine corn flake cereal, egg, barbecue sauce,
salt and pepper; beat until thoroughly mixed. Add ground beef.
Mix and shape into patties and place in 13"x9" baking dish. Bake
at 375 degrees for 25 minutes. Makes 3 servings.

Treasures of childhood, memories of old,
placed in a box, for stories yet told.

-Anonymous

Grilled Ham Steak

Nancy Wisc
Little Rock, AR

Glazed with a tangy, sweet sauce...this is the best!

1/4 c. apricot preserves
1 T. mustard
1 t. lemon juice

1/8 t. cinnamon
2-lb. ham steak

Blend together preserves, mustard, lemon juice and cinnamon. Cook over low heat, stirring constantly, until thoroughly combined, about 3 minutes; set aside. Grill ham steak over medium heat for 8 to 10 minutes per side. Brush with glaze during last few minutes of grilling. Serves 6.

Growing up, my brother and I were quite a pair.

Hometown Diner

Upside-Down Meat Loaf

Nancy Bigham
New Paris, OH

I've been making this recipe for 30 or 35 years. It's always a hit at family reunions because it is so unusual and tasty!

1-1/2 lbs. ground beef
2/3 c. evaporated milk
1/4 c. fine bread crumbs
1/4 c. chili sauce
1/4 c. onion, chopped
2-1/2 t. salt, divided
1/8 t. pepper

2 to 3 tomatoes, peeled and
   thickly sliced
1-1/3 c. instant rice, uncooked
2 T. fresh parsley, chopped
1/4 t. dried basil
1-1/4 c. water

Combine beef, milk, bread crumbs, chili sauce, onion, 1-1/2 teaspoon salt and pepper; mix well. Arrange tomatoes in the bottom of a pan or round 2-quart baking dish. Sprinkle rice, parsley, remaining salt and basil over the tomatoes. Pour water over the rice and tomatoes; cover with meat loaf mixture. Bake at 350 degrees for one hour or until meat loaf is cooked throughout. Remove from oven and let stand for 5 minutes, then invert over serving platter. Makes 8 to 10 servings.

"After chores were done, we and the neighborhood kids would ride our bikes, play flashlight tag, hide and seek and light sparklers. I remember almost every night ended with a cool treat of ice cream or watermelon!"

Jody Sinkula
Dresser, WI

Beefy Biscuit Casserole

Elizabeth Ramicone
Dublin, OH

A simple dish that your whole family will love.

1/2 c. celery, chopped
1/4 c. onion, chopped
1/4 c. green pepper, chopped
1 lb. ground beef
1-lb. can pork and beans
1/4 c. catsup
1/4 c. water

1 t. salt, divided
1/2 t. garlic salt
1 c. all-purpose flour
1-1/2 t. baking powder
1/3 c. milk
3 T. oil

Place celery, onion and green pepper in the bottom of an 8"x8 baking dish. Crumble ground beef on top. Bake at 425 degrees, uncovered, for 20 minutes. Blend in pork and beans, catsup, water, 1/2 teaspoon salt and garlic salt with ground beef. Return baking dish to oven for 10 minutes. Sift together flour, baking powder and remaining salt. In another mixing bowl, whisk together milk and oil; add to dry ingredients. Using a fork, stir until dough forms. Knead dough on a lightly floured surface for one minute. Roll out to 1/4-inch thickness, cut with a biscuit cutter. Arrange biscuits over ground beef in baking dish. Return to oven and bake an additional 15 to 20 minutes longer, until golden. Makes 6 to 8 servings.

Remember when the families would pull their chairs close to the radio and listen to thrilling radio shows? You can still rent the great classics on cassette or compact disc at your local library! Pick some up and relive the magic of old-fashioned radio!

Cranberry Pork Roast

Andrea Purdon
Redding, CA

Slices of tender pork roast, steamed potatoes and homemade stuffing make this a meal everyone will rush to the table for!

2-1/2 to 3-lbs. boneless, rolled
    pork loin roast
16-oz. can jellied cranberry
    sauce
1/2 c. sugar
1/2 c. cranberry juice

1 t. dry mustard
1/4 t. ground cloves
2 T. cornstarch
2 T. cold water
salt to taste

Place pork roast in a slow cooker. In a medium bowl, mash cranberry sauce; stir in sugar, cranberry juice, mustard and cloves. Pour over roast. Cover and cook on low for 6 to 8 hours or until meat is tender. Remove roast and keep warm. Skim fat from juices; discard. Add broth to a 2-cup measuring cup, adding water if necessary to equal 2 cups total liquid. Pour in saucepan and bring to a boil over medium-high heat. Combine cornstarch and cold water to make a paste; stir into saucepan. Cook and stir until thickened. Season with salt. Serve over sliced pork. Makes 4 to 6 servings.

Just about every county has a fair to show off the best they have, so spend a day at your hometown's fair. You'll discover terrific things...beautiful handmade quilts, displays of prize-winning produce, rows of colorful canned goods and some of the best food ever!

Potato, Ham & Cheese Bake

Bobbi Carney
Aurora, CO

After I had my first son, a friend shared this delicious casserole with our family...we've loved it ever since!

2 c. cooked ham, cubed
14 oz. frozen O'Brien hash
   browns
3 T. butter
10-oz. pkg. frozen corn
3 T. all-purpose flour
1-1/2 c. milk

1/2 t. Worcestershire sauce
1/2 t. dry mustard
1/4 t. salt
1/4 t. pepper
1 c. Cheddar cheese, grated
1/4 c. bread crumbs

Brown ham and hash browns in butter. Add corn, flour, milk, Worcestershire sauce, mustard, salt and pepper. Heat until sauce thickens. Spoon into a 9"x9" baking dish, add cheese and top with bread crumbs. Bake, uncovered, at 375 degrees for 30 minutes. Serves 4 to 6.

Twirling my baton during those crisp, Friday night football games was always the best!

Hometown Diner

Country Green Beans & Sausage

Sandy Dodson
Indianapolis, IN

Whenever we have reunions or get-togethers, everyone wants to know "Where are the green beans?"

3 slices bacon, crisply cooked
   and crumbled, 1 T. drippings
   reserved
3 14-1/2 oz. cans green beans,
   liquid reserved

3 15-oz. cans round, white
   potatoes, drained
1 onion, quartered
salt and pepper to taste
2-lbs. smoked sausage, sliced

Combine green beans, potatoes, onion, salt and pepper in a large Dutch oven. Cook on medium-low for approximately 45 minutes. Add reserved bacon drippings and sausage to the green beans. Continue cooking over medium-low heat for 30 minutes. Add bacon to the green beans. Makes 6 servings.

"Each year my husband and I would attend the Irrigation Festival in Sequim, Washington. Before the parade began, the national anthem was played. Almost in unison, everyone, from the very young to senior citizens removed their hats and placed them over their hearts. It was so heartwarming to see such patriotism."

Anne Olson
Sequim, WA

Sour Cream-Chicken Casserole

Windy Houser
Deltona, FL

After every potluck dinner, I always have an empty casserole dish to take home. It is so simple to make and so delicious to taste!

8-oz. pkg. stuffing mix, divided
1 stick butter, melted and
   divided
8 oz. sour cream
10-3/4 oz. can cream of chicken
   soup

10-3/4 oz. can cream of celery
   soup
4 to 6 boneless, skinless chicken
   breasts, cooked and cubed

Layer half of stuffing mix and half of butter in the bottom of a 2-quart casserole dish. In a medium bowl, mix sour cream and soups; spoon over stuffing. Top sour cream mixture with chicken. In a medium bowl, mix together remaining stuffing and butter; spread over chicken. Bake at 350 degrees for 45 minutes. Makes 6 to 8 servings.

Invite neighbors over to share a cold, frosty
glass of lemonade on the porch.

Hometown Diner

Family Swiss Steak

Marie Alana Gardner
North Tonawanda, NY

Almost like a pot roast, this would be tasty with a side of noodles!

1-1/2 lbs. round steak
3 T. all-purpose flour
1 T. fresh parsley, chopped
1/4 t. dried thyme
1/8 t. pepper

2 T. oil
1/2 c. onion, sliced
2 carrots, cut in strips
10-3/4 oz. can French onion
   soup

With a meat mallet, pound steak to 1/4-inch thickness; cut into pieces. In a 9" pie plate, stir together flour, parsley, thyme and pepper. Coat steak with flour mixture. In a 10" skillet, heat oil. Add steak and brown over medium heat, about 3 to 4 minutes on each side; add remaining ingredients. Reduce heat to low; cover and continue cooking for an additional 50 to 60 minutes. Makes 4 servings.

Apothecary jars give a nostalgic feel no matter where you use them, and they're just right for gift-giving, too. Fill them with sugar or flour, tuck in a scoop and give to a friend who loves to bake. Cotton balls, baby wipes and pacifiers will be close at hand for a new mom, or jars of buttons, thread and thimbles for a seamstress!

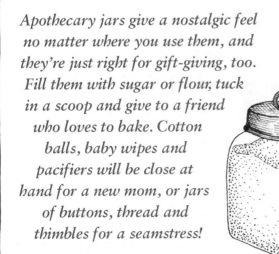

Cranberry Meat Loaves

Jodi Zarnoth-Hirsch
Chilton, WI

Individual meat loaves for each member of the family!

1 lb. ground beef
1 c. rice, cooked
1/2 c. tomato juice
1 egg
1/4 c. onion, minced

1 t. salt
16-oz. can whole cranberry
  sauce
1/3 c. brown sugar, packed
1 T. lemon juice

Mix beef, rice, tomato juice, egg, onion and salt together. Shape into 5 mini meat loaves and place in a 13"x9" pan. Mix together cranberry sauce, brown sugar and lemon juice; spoon over top of each loaf. Bake at 350 degrees for 45 minutes. Makes 5 servings.

"Our family's annual trip to the state fair in late summer was always fun. I remember Grandpa would bet me he could drink more milk than I could at the "all-you-can-drink milk booth!" Often it was a close contest, but Grandpa always won. Mom would laughingly exclaim it was the only time I would drink milk without an argument."

Linda Haiby
Andover, MN

Barbecued Pork Chops

Sandra Seymour
Taylor, MI

A change of pace, these are brushed with a sweet-hot glaze!

1 T. oil
1/2 c. onion, chopped
1/2 c. celery, chopped
1 c. catsup
1-1/2 c. molasses
1/2 c. water

2 t. dry mustard
1/4 t. salt
2 T. red wine vinegar
1/4 t. cayenne pepper
6 pork chops

Heat oil in a medium saucepan. Add onion and celery and cook over medium-low heat for 5 minutes. Stir in catsup, molasses, water, mustard, salt, vinegar and pepper; mix well. Bring to a boil; reduce heat and simmer for 15 minutes, stirring occasionally. Place pork chops on broiler pan 5 inches from heat. Broil for about 8 minutes on each side, brushing often with sauce. Makes 6 servings.

On warm days, Mom always loaded the car
with picnic goodies and we headed out to
the park...I could hardly wait!

Macaroni & Cheese

Kim Henry
Library, PA

*What could be better than a big bowl of
homemade macaroni & cheese?*

8-oz. pkg. elbow macaroni,
  cooked
3/4 c. mayonnaise
1/4 c. onion, chopped
10-3/4 oz. can cream of
  mushroom soup

1/2 lb. Cheddar cheese, grated
2 T. butter
10 to 12 round, buttery crackers,
  crumbled

In a 2-quart casserole dish, mix the macaroni with the mayonnaise,
onion, soup and Cheddar cheese. In a mixing bowl, combine butter
and crackers; spread over the macaroni mixture. Bake, uncovered, at
350 degrees for 30 minutes. Serves 4.

*Using a collection of colorful
dinnerware can bring back the
feel of an old time diner to
any kitchen and it's so easy!
Set your table with plates,
bowls and cups in bright
colors, then look for
sets of vintage
silverware. Lots of the
old-style patterns were
made with handles in
fun colors, too!*

Hometown Diner

One-Dish Tuna & Noodles

Tina Wright
Atlanta, GA

One of those simple dishes we all remember from childhood.

10-3/4 oz. can cream of
    mushroom soup
2/3 c. water
2 t. chopped pimentos

4 oz. American cheese, sliced
7-oz. can tuna, drained
4 oz. egg noodles, cooked

In a medium saucepan, blend together soup and water. Over medium heat, cook and stir constantly until smooth. Fold in pimentos and cheese; stir until cheese melts. Remove from heat and set aside. Combine tuna and noodles; spoon into a shallow 2-quart baking dish. Pour cheese mixture on top; gently stir. Bake at 375 degrees for 30 minutes. Makes 6 servings.

*Tag sales are great places to find tin picnic baskets
and they have so many uses! Fill one with a thermos of chicken
noodle soup and a loaf of homemade bread for a friend who's
under the weather, or pack it with an assortment of cookies and
mail to a college student away from home.*

Spaghetti Sauce & Meatballs

Karen Pilcher
Burleson, TX

This recipe has been in our family for years.

1/4 c. plus 2 T. olive oil, divided
2 onions, chopped
2 cloves garlic, divided
3/4 lb. mushrooms, sliced
1 T. plus 1 t. salt, divided
1/2 t. plus 1/8 t. pepper, divided
1 green pepper, minced
28-oz. can whole tomatoes,
    chopped and undrained
12-oz. can tomato paste

1-1/4 c. water
1 T. sugar
6 whole cloves
1 bay leaf
4 slices dry bread
1 lb. ground beef
1/2 c. grated Parmesan cheese
2 T. fresh parsley, chopped
1 t. dried oregano
2 lbs. spaghetti, cooked

Heat 1/4 cup oil in a heavy skillet. Add onions, one clove garlic and mushrooms. Cook over medium heat for 15 minutes, stirring occasionally. Add one tablespoon salt, 1/2 teaspoon pepper, green pepper, tomatoes, tomato paste, water, sugar, cloves and bay leaf. Simmer, uncovered, for one hour, stirring occasionally. Remove garlic, cloves and bay leaf; set sauce aside. Soak bread in water for 2 to 3 minutes, then squeeze out moisture. Combine bread, remaining garlic, salt, pepper, ground beef, Parmesan cheese, parsley and oregano; form into balls. Grease a jelly roll pan with remaining oil and place meatballs in it. Bake at 350 degrees for 30 minutes or until lightly browned. Drain on paper towels and add to spaghetti sauce during the last 30 minutes of cooking. Serve over spaghetti. Makes 6 servings.

Look for old postcards of your hometown at flea markets
or antique shops. They're inexpensive and such fun
to spread out on a table top or trunk lid!
Don't forget to cover them with a piece of glass
cut to fit, so they'll stay protected.

Hometown Diner

Lasagna

DeNeane Deskins
Indian Harbor Beach, FL

You can be sure everyone will be at the dinner table on time for this!

1/2 lb. ground beef
1/2 lb. Italian sausage, chopped
1 clove garlic, minced
2 T. Italian seasoning
1-lb. can Italian stewed
    tomatoes
2 6-oz. cans tomato paste
1 onion, diced

2 eggs
3 c. ricotta cheese
1/2 c. grated Parmesan cheese
salt and pepper to taste
2 T. parsley flakes
10 oz. lasagna noodles, cooked
1 lb. mozzarella cheese,
    shredded

In a skillet, brown beef and sausage; drain. Add garlic, Italian seasoning, tomatoes, tomato paste and onion; simmer. In a large bowl, mix eggs, ricotta, Parmesan, salt, pepper and parsley. In a 13"x9" baking pan, layer noodles, cheese mixture, meat sauce, mozzarella cheese; repeat layers until pan is filled, being sure to end with mozzarella cheese. Cover with aluminum foil and bake at 350 degrees for 45 minutes to one hour. Makes 6 to 8 servings.

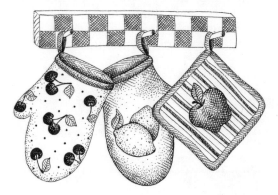

Almost everyone loves pizza, so why not provide the crust and sauce, then invite friends to visit and share their favorite toppings? Who knows, you might create a new combination!

Potato-Topped Chicken à la King

Nichole Kuklinski
Stevens Point, WI

Try this twist on an old favorite!

5 T. butter, divided
1/4 c. green onions, chopped
1/3 c. all-purpose flour
3/4 t. salt, divided
1/8 t. pepper
14-1/2 oz. can chicken broth
1-1/4 c. milk, divided
2 c. chicken, cooked and cubed

1/2 c. mushrooms, chopped
1 c. frozen baby sweet peas
1-1/2 c. water
1 t. garlic, minced
2-1/4 c. potato flakes
1 egg
Garnish: paprika and 2 T. green
    onions, chopped

Melt 2 tablespoons butter in a large skillet over medium heat. Add green onions; cook and stir for one minute. Add flour, 1/2 teaspoon salt and pepper; stir until blended. Gradually add broth and 1/2 cup milk; cook until boiling and mixture thickens, stirring constantly. Add chicken, mushrooms and peas; mix well. Spoon into an ungreased 8"x8" baking dish. In a medium saucepan, combine water, remaining butter, salt and garlic; bring to a boil. Remove from heat; stir in potato flakes and remaining milk. Add egg; mix well and spoon around the edges and over the chicken mixture in the baking dish. Garnish with paprika and green onions. Bake at 350 degrees for 30 minutes or until casserole is bubbly and top is lightly golden. Makes 4 servings.

Keep your camera close by to capture the kids in all their "firsts." Photos of a first haircut or first day of school will become sweet reminders as they grow up.

Double Cheese & Bacon Pie

*Rita Morgan
Pueblo, CO*

If you want to make this ahead, just cool completely, store in an airtight container and freeze for up to a month.

1-1/3 c. all-purpose flour
1/8 t. salt
1 stick chilled butter, sliced
2 to 3 T. cold water
4 eggs
1-1/2 c. light cream
1/4 t. dried thyme

1/8 t. white pepper
10 slices bacon, crisply cooked
   and crumbled
1/2 c. Gruyére cheese, shredded
1/2 c. white Cheddar cheese,
   shredded

Sift together flour and salt; cut in butter until coarse crumbs form. Add water, one tablespoon at a time, tossing with a fork, until a dough forms. Wrap dough in plastic wrap and refrigerate for 30 minutes. Roll dough on a lightly floured surface into an 11-inch circle. Turn into a 9" pie pan letting 1/4 inch hang over the pie pan edges. Fold dough under and crimp. Using a fork, prick dough and bake at 375 degrees for 10 to 15 minutes, or until lightly golden. Set aside to cool. In a small bowl, whisk together the eggs, cream, thyme and pepper. Pour into crust. Sprinkle with the bacon and cheeses. Bake at 375 degrees for 30 minutes, or until center is set. Serves 8.

All the little girls in your neighborhood would love to receive an invitation to a tea party. Fill a trunk with hats, gloves and costume jewelry and let everyone choose something to wear…what fun they'll have playing "dress up!" Serve pretty cut-out cookies and tiny cakes with pitchers of lemonade and milk.

Sausage Casserole

Rosalie Benson
Coats, NC

I grew up enjoying sausage and sauerkraut as did my husband. However, our 3 children would eat the sausage but never the sauerkraut. The addition of the brown sugar, apples and spices enticed them to give it a try and now...when they visit, they frequently suggest that I cook this easy dish for them.

2 to 3 T. brown sugar, packed
1 to 2 t. caraway seeds
1/4 t. ground cloves
16-oz. jar sauerkraut, drained
16-oz. can sliced potatoes,
    drained

2 apples, peeled, cored and
    chopped
16 oz. fully-cooked Polish
    sausage, chopped

Mix brown sugar, caraway seeds, cloves and sauerkraut in a 4-quart casserole dish. Gently stir in potatoes, apples and sausage. Bake in a 350 degree oven for 30 minutes. Makes 4 servings.

Summer days at the ball park. Hitting a home run made this the biggest game of the year!

Turkey Amandine

Sharon Hill
Roanoke, IL

My great-uncle Fletcher gave me this recipe and it never fails to get rave reviews whenever I serve it.

3 c. turkey, cooked and cubed
10-3/4 oz. can cream of chicken
   soup
1/2 c. sour cream
1/3 c. mayonnaise
1/2 c. celery, diced
1/3 c. onion, diced
8-oz. can sliced water chestnuts,
   drained

4-oz. can sliced mushrooms,
   drained
8-oz. tube refrigerated crescent
   rolls
3 T. butter, melted
4 oz. slivered almonds
3/4 c. Swiss or Cheddar cheese,
   shredded

In a saucepan, mix turkey, soup, sour cream, mayonnaise, celery, onion, water chestnuts and mushrooms until bubbly. Place in a greased 13"x9" pan. Unroll crescent rolls and place on top of turkey mixture. Mix together butter, almonds and cheese; spoon mixture evenly over top of dough. Bake at 375 degrees for 20 to 25 minutes. Makes 8 servings.

"I remember learning how to ride a bike, play hop-scotch and jump rope on our hometown street. Each season holds a favorite memory…in spring I would roller skate, then in summer, wait for the chimes of the ice cream truck to ring each evening. A nearby hill was the perfect spot to watch an autumn ball game, then in winter the same hill was great for sledding. I had a lot of fun without ever leaving our street."

Kathleen Macchione
Upper Arlington, OH

Reuben Casserole

Patricia Empson
Traverse City, MI

Cheesy and yummy! Try this for your next get-together.

8 oz. wide egg noodles, cooked
4 T. butter, divided
1 lb. sauerkraut
12 oz. corned beef, diced
2 c. Swiss cheese, shredded

1 tomato, sliced
1/2 c. Thousand Island dressing
1/2 c. bread crumbs
1/2 t. caraway seeds

Toss noodles with 2 tablespoons butter, sauerkraut and corned beef. Lightly toss in cheese and spread in a 13"x9" casserole dish. Layer tomato slices on top and cover with dressing. Brown bread crumbs and caraway seeds in remaining butter and sprinkle on top of casserole. Bake at 350 degrees for one hour. Makes 6 servings.

"In the winter, Mom, Dad, my brothers, sisters and I would go in the backyard and pack down the newly fallen snow until it was flat. After running a watering hose out from the basement and wetting the entire area, the next day it would be frozen so we could skate! We'd stay outside until it was too cold and then all tumble into the kitchen, pulling off skates, mittens and scarves to enjoy popcorn and drink hot chocolate to warm up."

Maureen Baly
Sylvan Lake, IL

Slow Cooker Beef & Noodles

Shirley Allen
Indianapolis, IN

I make mashed potatoes and top them with beef and noodles.

2 lbs. stew beef
2 10-1/2 oz. cans beef broth
2 c. water

1-1/2 T. Italian seasoning
2 12-oz. pkgs. egg noodles,
   uncooked

In a slow cooker, place stew beef, broth, water and Italian seasoning. Cook on high for 4 hours or on low for 8 hours. Place noodles in slow cooker for the last hour of cooking.

Organize a block party and bring neighbors together for some fun! First, you'll need to check with your local police department to see if you need a permit, then just set a date. Ask each family to bring a main dish for their family, plus a dish to share. Gather together several grills so everyone can cook without missing all the fun!

Broccoli-Ham Ring

Jane Powers
Chippewa Falls, WI

One of my favorites...very tasty and so pretty.

2 8-oz. tubes refrigerated
   crescent rolls
4 oz. cooked ham, chopped
1/4 lb. broccoli, chopped
1 onion, chopped

1/4 c. fresh parsley, snipped
6 oz. Cheddar or Swiss cheese,
   shredded
2 T. Dijon mustard
1 T. lemon juice

Unroll crescent dough and separate into triangles. Arrange the triangles with the wide ends overlapping and the narrow ends falling over the edge of a 12" pizza pan; this should form a sunburst design with the center open. Gently press the overlapping areas down. Mix ham, broccoli, onion, parsley, cheese, mustard and lemon juice together. Spread filling onto crescent ring. Bring narrow ends of dough over the filling and tuck underneath center hole forming a wreath shape. Bake at 350 degrees for 30 to 35 minutes.
Makes 8 servings.

"Every 4th of July was an event for our
family. Mother made fried chicken, salads
and all the trimmings and Dad was in charge
of the fireworks. Grandpa brought everything
needed for root beer floats, which was
always a family tradition, and we could have
as many as our tummies could hold!"

Sylvia Mathews
Vancouver, WA

Hometown Diner

Oven-Fried Chicken

Janet Pastrick
Gooseberry Patch

Just right for a family picnic! Fill your basket with chicken, macaroni salad, potato chips, fresh veggies and a thermos of lemonade!

1 egg, beaten
1/2 c. milk
1 c. all-purpose flour
2 T. chopped pecans
1 t. baking powder

2 t. salt
2 T. sesame seed
2-1/2 to 3 lbs. chicken,
   quartered
1/4 lb. butter, melted

In a medium bowl, combine egg and milk. In a separate bowl, mix together flour, pecans, baking powder, salt and sesame seeds. Take pieces of chicken and dip first in egg mixture, then in flour mixture, coating well. Drizzle with butter and place on a baking platter with skin side up. Bake at 400 degrees for 30 minutes. Turn chicken over and cook until tender and golden. Makes 4 servings.

Lazy summer days...I can't believe we all fit on Grandma's porch swing!

Slow Cooker Smothered Steak

Lynda McCormick
Burkburnett, TX

The meat is so tender it just falls apart!

1/3 c. all-purpose flour
1 t. garlic salt
1/2 t. pepper
1-1/2 lbs. round steak, cut into
    strips
1 onion, sliced
2 green peppers, sliced

4-oz. can sliced mushrooms,
    drained
10-oz. pkg. frozen French-style
    green beans
4 T. soy sauce
9 c. white rice, cooked

Mix flour, garlic salt and pepper together; place in a plastic bag. Place steak in plastic bag with flour mixture; shake to coat. Remove steak from plastic bag and add to slow cooker. Layer onion, green peppers, mushrooms and green beans over steak. Pour soy sauce over all. Cover and cook on high for one hour; reduce to low for 8 hours. Serve over white rice. Makes 6 servings.

Arrange your favorite high school photos, postcards, pennants and pressed flowers in an 17" x11" frame. Attach handles to the short sides of the frame and you'll have a wonderful tray filled with memories!

Turkey Tetrazzini

Sandy Durham
Wichita Falls, TX

You can easily substitute chicken for turkey...either way it's terrific!

6 T. margarine, melted and
    divided
1 onion, diced
1/4 c. all-purpose flour
2-3/4 c. milk
1 cube chicken bouillon

1/2 t. salt
1/4 c. grated Parmesan cheese
4 slices bread, torn in bite-size
    pieces
8 oz. spaghetti, cooked
2 c. turkey, cooked and cubed

In saucepan, over medium heat, melt 3 tablespoons margarine
and cook onion until tender. Stir in flour until blended. Gradually
stir in milk, bouillon and salt. Cook, stirring until slightly thick.
Remove from heat and stir in cheese. In small saucepan, over low
heat, melt remaining margarine and mix in bread. Place spaghetti in
13"x9" baking dish, add sauce and turkey. Gently toss to mix and top
with torn bread. Bake, uncovered, at 350 degrees for 30 minutes.
Makes 8 servings.

*Feed sacks from the 1940's
are fun to collect!
Drape them over a
wooden drying rack for
an instant room divider,
or lay one over
a tension rod for a bright
kitchen valance!*

Baked Chicken & Noodles

Liz Plotnick
Gooseberry Patch

A great homestyle dish that everyone will love.

3 T. butter, melted
1 t. paprika
3/4 t. dried marjoram
1/2 t. lemon zest
1/2 t. pepper
2-1/2 lbs. chicken, cubed

4 c. broad egg noodles,
    uncooked
1-1/4 c. chicken broth
1 T. cornstarch
1/2 c. grated Parmesan cheese
1 T. dried parsley

Blend together butter, paprika, marjoram, zest and pepper. Arrange chicken pieces in a single layer in ungreased 13"x9" baking dish; pour butter mixture over chicken. Bake, uncovered, at 375 degrees for 45 to 50 minutes. Cook noodles according to package directions; drain. Remove chicken from baking dish, set aside; reserve drippings. Stir together drippings, broth and cornstarch in a saucepan. Bring to a boil, stirring constantly, until mixture is thick and bubbly. Stir in noodles, cheese and parsley. Serve chicken over noodles. Serves 4 to 6.

"Many times our church had dinner outside. There were several tables loaded with made-from-scratch food. Granny would always bring the chicken & dumplings, which were the best in the world. Sometimes she would add just a drop of yellow food coloring to the dumplings for some color, but once she added red by mistake! Even though the chicken & dumplings were pink and there were lots of laughs, the wonderful taste was still the same!"

Robin Wilson
Altamonte Springs, FL

Hometown Diner

Easy Chicken Pot Pie

Meredith Wood
Dallas, TX

This will make your whole house smell delicious!

2 c. chicken, cooked and cubed
2 10-3/4 oz. cans cream of
    potato soup
15-oz. can mixed vegetables,
    drained
1/2 c. milk

1/2 t. dried thyme
pepper to taste
2 9-inch pie crusts, unbaked
1 egg yolk
2 t. water

Mix chicken, soup, vegetables, milk, thyme and pepper together; pour into pie crust. Add top crust, crimp edges to seal and cut slits so steam can vent. Blend egg yolk and water together, brush on top of pie crust for a glaze. Bake at 375 degrees for 40 minutes. Remove and cool for 10 minutes before serving. Serves 6 to 8.

Playing "Blind Man's Bluff" at the barn dance.

Chili Casserole

Michelle Campen
Peoria, IL

*I've been making this casserole for about 20 years and I seem
to always get requests to share the recipe.*

1 lb. ground beef
1 onion, diced
16-oz. can tomato sauce
1-1/4 oz. pkg. chili seasoning
   mix

1 c. water
3/4 c. Cheddar cheese, shredded
1-1/4 c. mozzarella cheese,
   shredded
2 c. corn chips, crushed

In frying pan, brown ground beef and onion. Add tomato sauce,
chili seasoning mix and water. Simmer 10 to 15 minutes, stirring
2 or 3 times. Layer ground beef mixture, cheeses and corn chips in
a 2-quart casserole dish; repeat layers ending with corn chips. Bake
at 350 degrees for 20 minutes. Makes 6 servings.

*Vintage painted, metal chairs look great scattered in your yard.
Their bright red, yellow and blue colors add a splash of fun!*

Hometown Diner

Cranberry-Orange Pork Chops

Jo Ann

The combination of tart cranberries and sweet orange is really a winner! It's ready in only an hour so it's great for a busy family.

6 pork chops
1-1/2 T. butter
1-1/2 T. oil
1 c. cranberries
juice of one orange

salt and pepper to taste
1/4 c. brown sugar, packed
1 T. all-purpose flour
1/2 c. water
Garnish: orange slices

Place pork chops in a skillet with butter and oil. Brown on both sides; drain drippings and discard. Stir in cranberries, orange juice, salt, pepper and brown sugar. Simmer, covered, for one hour. Blend together flour and water and pour in skillet. Cook, stirring often, until thickened. Pour sauce over pork chops and garnish with orange slices. Serves 4 to 6.

During autumn, the high school grandstand is always full for the Friday night football game, so cheer on your team! Pack a basket of goodies to enjoy while the marching band perform at halftime...crunchy apples, spicy molasses cookies and a thermos filled with warm cider would be just right.

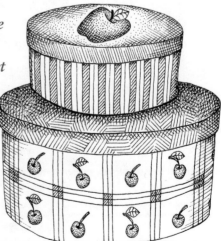

Honey-Mustard Chicken

Rogene Rogers
Bemidji, MN

*If you'd like, make some extra honey-mustard sauce
to serve along side for dipping.*

3 T. butter
6 to 8 boneless, skinless chicken
   breasts
1/4 c. honey

1/4 t. mustard
1 t. sugar
3 T. lemon juice

Melt butter in 13"x9" baking pan. Place chicken pieces in baking pan. Mix remaining ingredients together and spoon over chicken. Bake, uncovered, at 325 degrees for 30 minutes. Turn chicken to second side and bake for an additional hour or until golden. Continue basting with honey-mustard sauce while baking. Makes 6 to 8 servings.

*Neighborhood sales often turn
up vintage napkin or straw
dispensers, toothpick holders
or sugar and creamers.
Look for them in bright
color combinations,
like red and white, to
really give your
kitchen a hometown
diner feeling!*

Tomato-Basil Salad

Gail Prather
Bethel, MN

*If you have garden-fresh tomatoes and basil...this
is easy and delicious!*

4 tomatoes, cored and thinly
   sliced
salt and pepper to taste
1/4 c. olive oil, divided

2 T. white wine vinegar, divided
1/2 lb. feta cheese
1 c. fresh basil leaves, chopped
1/4 c. pine nuts

Place tomato slices on serving platter. Sprinkle with salt and pepper,
then drizzle on half of the olive oil and vinegar. Top with cheese, basil
and pine nuts. Add remaining oil and vinegar; marinate for 3 hours
before serving. Serve at room temperature. Makes 4 to 6 servings.

Pineapple Casserole

Sharon Chesley
North East, PA

Sensational with ham!

1/2 c. butter
3/4 c. sugar
3 eggs, beaten

20-oz. can crushed pineapple,
   drained
5 slices white bread, torn

Mix butter and sugar together. Add eggs, pineapple and bread. Mix
together and pour into an 8"x8" casserole dish. Bake at 325 degrees
for 45 minutes. Makes 4 to 6 servings.

*Give a little love to a child,
and you get a great deal back.*

-John Ruskin

Farmers' Market

Rice & Spinach Bake

Mary Anderson
San Bruno, CA

My mother has been making this recipe since 1960 and we all love it.
My grown sons and their families come home for visits
and if it doesn't appear, they are so disappointed.

10-oz. pkg. frozen, chopped
  spinach
1 c. rice, cooked
1 c. plus 1/2 c. sharp Cheddar
  cheese, shredded and divided

2 eggs
2 T. butter, softened
1/3 c. milk
1 onion, chopped
1/2 t. salt

Mix spinach, rice, one cup cheese, eggs, butter, milk, onion and salt together and pour into an 8"x8" casserole dish. Bake at 350 degrees for 20 minutes. Sprinkle remaining cheese over all and continue to bake an additional 5 minutes or until cheese melts. Makes 4 servings.

Lots of 4th of July festivities are held on the local town square... why not join in the fun? Pack a yummy picnic, sing along when the band plays, wave tiny flags and cheer for all the floats!

Garden Vegetable Casserole

Kathy Grashoff
Ft. Wayne, IN

*Use your fresh garden vegetables to make
this side dish even more tasty.*

1-1/2 c. rice, uncooked
5 tomatoes, sliced
3 zucchini, sliced
3 carrots, thinly sliced
2 green peppers, sliced into rings
1 onion, thinly sliced and
   separated into rings
3/4 c. water
6 T. olive oil
6 T. rice wine vinegar

3 T. fresh parsley, chopped
1 to 2 t. hot pepper sauce
2 cloves garlic, minced
1-1/2 t. salt
3/4 t. dried thyme
3/4 t. pepper
3/4 t. dried basil
1-1/2 c. mozzarella cheese,
   shredded
1/3 c. grated Parmesan cheese

Place 3/4 cup rice in each of two, 11"x7" baking dishes. Layer half of vegetables over rice in each dish. In a small bowl, combine water, oil, vinegar, parsley, pepper sauce, garlic, salt, thyme, pepper and basil; stir until well blended. Pour half of oil mixture over vegetables in each dish. Bake, covered, at 350 degrees for 1-1/2 hours or until vegetables are tender. Sprinkle cheeses over both casseroles and continue to bake, uncovered, for approximately 10 minutes or until cheese melts. Each baking dish makes 6 to 8 servings.

*Friends, books, a cheerful heart and a conscience clear
are the most choice companions we have here.*

-William Mather

Farmers' Market

Spinach & Mushroom Salad

Stephanie Swensen
Mapleton, UT

I get tons of requests for this salad at family get-togethers...the dressing is my favorite part!

3/4 T. poppy seeds
1/3 c. sugar
3/4 t. salt
1/3 t. dry mustard
1/3 c. apple cider vinegar
3/4 c. oil
1 red onion
1 bunch spinach, torn into
　bite-size pieces

1 head iceberg lettuce, torn into
　bite-size pieces
3/4 lb. mushrooms, sliced
3/4 lb. Swiss cheese, grated
3/4 lb. bacon, crisply cooked and
　crumbled
3 eggs, hard-boiled and diced

Place poppy seeds, sugar, salt, mustard, vinegar and oil in a blender.
Slice onion down the middle, dicing one half and slicing the remaining
half into rings. Place 3/4 tablespoon diced onion in blender with
vinegar mixture and pulse several times until onion is chopped.
Continue to blend for one to 2 minutes or until dressing is creamy.
Toss onion rings with all remaining ingredients in a large salad bowl.
Just before serving, shake dressing well and pour over salad; toss.
Makes 6 to 8 servings.

*It's fun to combine lots
of kitchenware and
fresh herbs and flowers.
Fill old-fashioned sifters,
enamelware pots and pans,
tea kettles or canning jars,
then set them in your
windowsill...easy
and so pretty!*

Marinated Vegetable Salad

Lorelei Campbell
Hampton, VA

Serve with burgers, fish or chicken for a yummy dinner!

1 c. sugar
1 t. salt
1 t. pepper
3/4 c. apple cider vinegar
1/2 c. oil
1/2 t. seasoned salt
1 T. water
10-oz. pkg. frozen peas, thawed
15-oz. can white shoepeg corn,
  drained

1 c. green pepper, chopped
4-oz. jar chopped pimentos
1 cucumber, chopped
14-1/2 oz. can green beans,
  drained
1 c. celery, chopped
1 c. onion, chopped
2 carrots, thinly sliced
2 tomatoes, chopped

In a saucepan, heat sugar, salt, pepper, vinegar, oil, seasoned salt and water until sugar dissolves; cool. Place vegetables into a large serving bowl and pour dressing over; refrigerate for 24 hours. Toss before serving. Makes 6 to 8 servings.

A summerime favorite in my neighborhood, fresh, juicy watermelon from the farm stand!

Farmers' Market

German Green Beans

Patricia Taylor
Wellsville, PA

My family loves this so much, there's never any left over!

2 14-1/2 oz. cans green beans,
    drained
15-1/4 oz. can corn, drained
1 t. seasoned salt
1 T. onion powder
1 clove garlic, minced
1 T. vinegar

4 to 5 T. olive oil
4 to 5 carrots, grated
1/2 t. dried dill weed
1/2 t. dried oregano
1/4 t. dried tarragon
5 slices bacon, crisply cooked
    and crumbled

Mix all ingredients, except bacon, together in a large serving bowl. Refrigerate overnight, stirring occasionally. Top with bacon and serve at room temperature. Makes 12 to 14 servings.

"Growing up in northern Illinois, Mr. and Mrs. Fleming lived across the street. Every summer, Mr. Fleming drove his truck across the Wisconsin border to a watermelon stand and filled it with huge, juicy watermelons! Before long, their yard was filled with dozens of neighbors and we all ate until we could burst, loving every minute of it!"

Teri Lindquist
Gurnee, IL

Parmesan Zucchini

Christine Petoff
Bremerton, WA

*A great alternative to zucchini bread when you are
harvesting zucchini at summer's end.*

2 zucchinis, sliced
1 roma tomato, diced
2 t. Worcestershire sauce
2 T. catsup
2 T. butter

1/8 t. salt
1/4 t. pepper
2 T. water
Garnish: fresh Parmesan cheese,
    grated

Place all ingredients into a saucepan; simmer for 10 to 15 minutes or
until tender. Garnish with Parmesan cheese. Makes 4 servings.

Coleslaw Delight

Terri Hansen
Goose Creek, SC

Crunchy with a sweet dressing!

2 3-oz. pkgs. ramen noodles
    with seasoning packet,
    noodles crushed
1/4 c. butter
1/3 c. sesame seeds
4 oz. sliced almonds
1 T. soy sauce

1/3 c. oil
1/4 t. sesame oil
1/4 c. rice wine vinegar
1/3 c. sugar
2 8-oz. pkgs. shredded coleslaw
2 bunches green onions,
    chopped

Brown noodles in butter with seasoning packet, sesame seeds and
almonds; cool. Mix soy sauce, oils, vinegar and sugar together;
refrigerate until ready to serve. Combine coleslaw, onions and
dressing. Toss with noodles before serving. Makes 4 to 6 servings.

Memories are like keepsakes...always to be treasured.

-Anonymous

Farmers' Market

A Little Different Macaroni Salad

Wanda Wilson
Hamilton, GA

Sweetened condensed milk is the secret ingredient!

16-oz. pkg. macaroni, cooked
4 carrots, grated
1 sweet onion, chopped
1/2 c. red pepper, chopped
1/2 c. green pepper, chopped
2 c. mayonnaise

14-oz. can sweetened condensed
  milk
1/4 to 1/2 c. sugar
1/2 c. white vinegar
salt and pepper to taste

Combine macaroni, carrots, onion and peppers in a large bowl. In a separate bowl, combine mayonnaise, milk, sugar and vinegar. Pour over macaroni and vegetables. Salt and pepper to taste. Chill at least 8 hours before serving to allow dressing to thicken. Mix well before serving. Makes 18 servings.

During the summer, there are lots of excuses for packing a lunch. Pile everyone in the car and head to a concert in the park or Little League game at the local ball park.

Amish Country Dressing

Connie Mossman
Newark, OH

Serve as a side dish or as a main dish, either way this is great!

18 slices dry bread, cubed
2 c. potatoes, diced and cooked
1 c. carrot, chopped
3 c. celery, chopped
1 onion, chopped
1 T. poultry seasoning

5 eggs, beaten
1 qt. warm chicken broth
2 sticks butter, melted
2 c. chicken, cooked and
    chopped
salt and pepper to taste

In a large bowl, place bread, potatoes, carrot, celery, onion and poultry seasoning; add eggs. Mix in chicken broth, butter and chicken; salt and pepper. Toss lightly and place in a greased 13"x9" pan. Bake, covered, at 375 degrees for 45 minutes. Remove cover and bake an additional 20 minutes. Makes 8 to 12 servings.

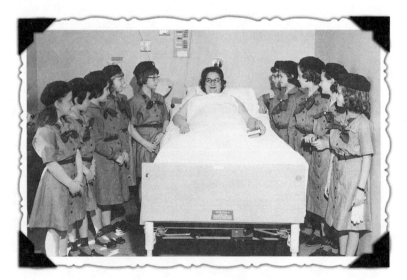

A surprise visit to our dear Brownie Troop Leader!

Farmers' Market

Cornbread Casserole

Angela Bettencourt
Mukilteo, WA

Just cut in squares and serve with a bowl of stew or chili.

2 onions, chopped
6 T. butter
2 eggs
2 T. milk
16-oz. pkg. corn muffin mix

2 14-3/4 oz. cans cream-style
   corn
1/2 pt. sour cream
2 c. Cheddar cheese, shredded

Sauté onions in butter; set aside. Mix together eggs and milk; add muffin mix and corn; blend well. Spread mixture into a greased 13"x9" baking dish. Top with onions, evenly spread on sour cream and sprinkle with cheese. Bake at 425 degrees for 35 minutes or until puffed and golden. Let sit 10 minutes before serving. Makes 6 to 8 servings.

"I remember a trip to visit our Brownie Leader, Mrs. London, in the hospital. Her husband was a doctor in our town, so as a surprise, we got dressed up in our Brownie finery and stopped in for a visit. It was our "get well" present to her!"

Donna Cozzens
Gooseberry Patch

Orange Salad

Terrianne Grant
Sewickley, PA

Being a mom of four, I'm always looking for easy and refreshing recipes; this salad fits the bill!

5 c. red leaf lettuce, torn
1 red onion, thinly sliced
2 stalks celery, sliced
11-oz. can mandarin oranges,
    drained
1/4 c. slivered almonds

1/4 c. balsamic vinegar
1/3 c. peanut oil
1/2 c. sugar
1 T. Dijon mustard
1/8 t. salt

Toss lettuce, onion, celery, oranges and almonds together in a large serving bowl. In a mixing bowl, whisk together vinegar, oil, sugar, mustard and salt. Pour over lettuce mixture. Makes 6 to 8 servings.

Serve icy pink lemonade, homemade root beer, or milk in 1950's jelly glasses. Lots of times you can find individual glasses at yard sales and sometimes tag sales, or antique shops have sets of four or six…perfect for a picnic!

Farmers' Market

Old-Time Fruit Salad

Jan Mansueto
Schererville, IN

*This very old recipe was given to me by one of
my quilt guild members!*

3 eggs, beaten
3/4 c. sugar
3 T. butter
1/2 c. lemon juice
3 Golden Delicious apples,
   peeled, cored and chopped
3 Red Delicious apples, peeled,
   cored and chopped

1 bunch green, seedless grapes,
   halved
1 bunch red, seedless grapes,
   halved
20-oz. can pineapple tidbits,
   drained
1-1/2 c. whole pecans
1-1/2 c. mini marshmallows

In a saucepan, combine eggs, sugar and butter; stir in lemon juice.
Heat until thickened, stirring constantly; refrigerate until cool. In a
large serving bowl, place fruit, pecans and marshmallows. Pour
dressing over fruit mixture; mix well. Serves 8 to 10.

*A weekend in the kitchen can
give you rows and rows
of home-canned goodies!
Invite friends over to
share your garden
bounty by canning
together. The day goes
so much faster when
you can laugh and
chat together!*

Red-Skinned Potato Salad

Wendye Sumner
Corpus Christi, TX

Try this variation that uses red potatoes...no need to peel!

3 lbs. red potatoes, cooked and
    chopped
12-oz. jar roasted red peppers,
    drained and chopped
12 green onions, sliced
fresh cilantro to taste

1/2 c. lime juice
1/3 c. olive oil
3/4 t. salt
1/2 t. pepper
4 avocados, peeled and cubed

In a large bowl, combine potatoes, red peppers, onions and cilantro. In a separate bowl, whisk together lime juice, oil, salt and pepper; add avocado and toss. Combine avocado mixture with potato mixture; toss gently. Cover and chill before serving. Makes 8 servings.

"I have wonderful memories of the local dimestore, with its large oak doors and wooden floors that creaked with every step. I'd always look at all the sweets in the large glass cases with childlike excitement, but my favorite part of the store were the bins that were filled with toys!"

Shari Cockerham
Seymour, IN

Farmers' Market

Country Potato Bake

Penny Frazier
Kokomo, IN

Guaranteed to be a hit!

1-lb. pkg. frozen hash browns
10-3/4 oz. can cream of chicken
   soup
8 oz. sour cream
4 T. margarine, melted

1 c. mild Cheddar cheese,
   shredded
6 slices bacon, crisply cooked
   and chopped
2.8-oz. can French fried onions

Spread hash browns evenly in the bottom of a greased 13"x9" baking dish. Mix together soup, sour cream and margarine. Pour soup mixture over hash browns. Sprinkle with cheese, bacon and onions. Bake, covered, at 350 degrees for 45 minutes. Makes 12 servings.

Shoepeg Corn Casserole

Jan Stafford
Trenton, GA

We double and sometimes triple this casserole for our large family.
It's great with Easter ham or any special occasion.

1/2 c. onion, chopped
1/2 c. celery, chopped
1 stick plus 2 T. butter, divided
14-1/2 oz. can French-style
   green beans, drained
15-oz. can shoepeg corn,
   drained

10-3/4 oz. can cream of celery
   soup
8 oz. sour cream
3/4 sleeve round, buttery
   crackers, crumbled
1/2 c. Cheddar cheese, grated
5-oz. pkg. sliced almonds

Sauté onion and celery together in 2 tablespoons butter. Mix together beans, corn, soup, onion, celery and sour cream. In a separate bowl, combine crackers, cheese, almonds and remaining butter together and top vegetable mixture. Bake at 350 degrees for about 40 minutes. Makes 6 to 8 servings.

Cauliflower Au Gratin

Erin Blaisure
Montrose, PA

If you're planning a family reunion, this dish feeds a crowd!

1 onion, diced
6 T. butter
6 T. all-purpose flour
6 c. milk
1 lb. American cheese, shredded
salt and pepper to taste

2 16-oz. pkgs. thawed, chopped
   cauliflower
3 T. bread crumbs
1 T. butter, melted
Garnish: fresh parsley, chopped

Sauté onion in butter until onion is transparent; blend in flour and milk, whisk and continue to stir until mixture becomes thick. Add cheese, stirring until cheese is melted and smooth; salt and pepper to taste. Gently fold cauliflower and cheese mixture into an ungreased 13"x9" casserole dish. Stir bread crumbs into melted butter; place on top of cauliflower mixture. Sprinkle parsley over all and bake at 350 degrees for 30 minutes. Makes 20 servings.

My first trick-or-treat! Mom held my hand from house to house, all the way around the block!

Farmers' Market

Sweet & Sour Broccoli Salad

Charlotte Wolfe
Fort Lauderdale, FL

You really could add any of your favorites to this recipe...sunflower seeds, cauliflower or shredded Cheddar cheese would be tasty.

1 bunch broccoli, chopped
1 red onion, sliced
4 to 5 slices bacon, crisply
    cooked and crumbled

1/4 c. golden raisins
3/4 c. mayonnaise
1/2 c. sugar
2 T. vinegar

Place broccoli, onion, bacon and raisins in a large serving bowl. In a separate bowl, combine mayonnaise, sugar and vinegar; stir together. Pour dressing over broccoli mixture just before serving; toss gently. Makes 6 servings.

"Each Halloween our town held a costume parade at dusk...everyone was invited to march through the center of town; even pets were in costumes! The highlight at the end of the day was always the bonfire where we'd enjoy powdered sugar doughnuts and cold apple cider".

Jan Bowden
Big Prairie, OH

Zucchini Hot Cakes

Phyllis Laughrey
Mount Vernon, OH

*Serve plain or topped with tomato sauce, grated cheese,
sour cream and chives!*

1-1/2 c. zucchini, grated
2 T. onion, finely chopped
1/4 c. grated Parmesan cheese
1/4 c. all-purpose flour
2 eggs

2 T. mayonnaise
1/4 t. dried oregano
salt and pepper to taste
1 T. butter

Mix together first 8 ingredients. Melt butter in a 10" skillet. Spoon about 2 tablespoons batter into skillet. Flatten with spoon. Cook over medium heat until golden, turn and cook second side. Repeat with remaining batter. Makes 2 to 3 servings.

*Nostalgic napkins, in colorful prints, make terrific
pillows for a porch swing! Just stitch 3 sides together,
slip in a pillow, then slip stitch the last side closed.*

Farmers' Market

Sunny Day Chicken Salad

Sherri Hunt
Garland, TX

Great for a light lunch.

1-oz. pkg. dry ranch dressing
  mix
1/2 c. mayonnaise
1/2 c. plain yogurt
1/4 c. honey
2 c. chicken, cooked and cubed
1/2 c. celery, sliced

8-oz. can pineapple chunks,
  drained
8-oz. can sliced water chestnuts,
  drained
1-1/2 c. red, seedless grapes,
  halved
1/2 c. slivered almonds, toasted
1 head lettuce, quartered

Mix together dressing mix, mayonnaise, yogurt and honey. Stir in chicken, celery, pineapple, water chestnuts, grapes and almonds; chill well. Spoon chicken salad in middle of each lettuce wedge. Makes 4 servings.

Make a star-spangled luminary! Use a star-shaped hole punch to decorate small brown lunch sacks or white bakery bags. Fill the bag with a little sand and then slip a tea light in a glass votive holder...perfect for lighting the way to your next get-together!

Spinach Noodle Salad

Lori Bourn
Lincoln, NE

*The spinach noodles and salami in this pasta salad make a
nice change from more traditional recipes.*

3/4 c. oil
1/4 c. Italian vinegar
1 t. mustard
1/8 t. pepper
3/8 t. garlic powder
3 T. plus 3/8 t. salt, divided
1/8 t. white pepper

10 qts. water
24 oz. green spinach noodles,
   uncooked
24 oz. salami, diced
1/2 c. onion, diced
1 c. grated Parmesan cheese

Place oil, vinegar, mustard, pepper, garlic powder, 3/8 teaspoon salt
and white pepper in a container with a tight fitting lid; shake until
spices are dissolved. In a large pot, bring water to a boil and add
remaining salt. Place noodles in boiling water for 3-1/2 minutes.
Rinse immediately with cold water. Drain noodles in colander for at
least 15 to 20 minutes to remove all excess moisture. Toss gently
several times during draining process. Place noodles, salami, onion
and Parmesan cheese in a mixing bowl. Add dressing and carefully
mix by hand. Refrigerate overnight. Toss before serving. Salad will
stay fresh 4 days. Makes 12 to 16 servings.

*...to lie sometimes on the grass
under trees on a summer's day,
listening to the murmur
of the water, or watching
the clouds float across
the sky is by no means
a waste of time.*

-Sir J. Lubbock

Farmers' Market

Scalloped Tomatoes

Nancy Bigham
New Paris, OH

The absolute best recipe I've ever found for scalloped tomatoes;
it was shared with me by a friend I used to work with.

4 slices bacon, crisply cooked
　　and crumbled, drippings
　　reserved
1 qt. canned tomatoes, drained

1/2 c. sugar
1 onion, diced
3 to 4 slices bread, cubed

Combine bacon, half of the reserved drippings, tomatoes, sugar, onion and bread cubes in a 2-quart casserole dish. Bake at 350 degrees for one hour. Makes 6 servings.

Strawberry & Spinach Salad

Catherine Smith
Champlin, MN

This refreshing and pretty salad is delicious.
A family favorite all-around!

1/2 lb. pecans
1 lb. spinach, torn
1 pt. strawberries, halved
1/3 c. red wine vinegar
1 t. salt

1/2 c. oil
1 t. dry mustard
1/2 c. sugar
1-1/2 t. onions, minced
1/2 t. poppy seeds

Brown pecans on a buttered baking sheet at 350 degrees for 10 minutes. In a large serving bowl, mix together spinach and strawberries. In a separate bowl, blend together vinegar, salt, oil, mustard, sugar, onion and poppy seeds. Add pecans to vinegar mixture; mix well. Gently stir dressing into spinach and strawberries before serving. Makes 8 to 10 servings.

Grandma's Special Green Beans

Brandi Glenn
Los Osos, CA

I make these green beans in honor of my grandmother who passed away when I was 12. My husband hates the fact that I only make these twice a year...but I tell him they wouldn't be as special if I made them all year long.

2 lbs. green beans, snapped into
    bite-size pieces
2 8-oz. cans tomato sauce
1 T. balsamic vinegar

8 slices bacon, crisply cooked
    and crumbled, 2 T. drippings
    reserved

Place all ingredients, including reserved drippings, in a 2-quart baking dish. Bake at 375 degrees for 30 minutes or until tender; stir twice during cooking time. Makes 6 servings.

My first kiss...from the girl next door!

Farmers' Market

Fruit Salad

Wanda Rogers
Kingwood, TX

My mother has made this salad for as long as I can remember.
It's a recipe that always brings back good memories!

3 Golden Delicious apples,
   peeled, cored and chopped
3 oranges, chopped
3 bananas, sliced
1/2 c. raisins

1 t. lemon juice
2 T. sugar
1/2 c. flaked coconut
1 c. chopped pecans
1/2 c. mayonnaise

In a large serving bowl, place apples, orange, bananas and raisins. In a separate bowl, mix together lemon juice, sugar, coconut, pecans and mayonnaise. Toss lemon juice mixture over fruit. Refrigerate until ready to serve. Makes 4 servings.

"I remember selling penny candy at the general store and the grade school children running down the hill at recess to buy it. They would press their noses and hands on the large glass front cases, eagerly scanning the candy looking for the best buy. Needless to say, the glass fronts always needed a cleaning after they left!"

Jo Baker
Litchfield, IL

Calico Beans

Heather Denk
Naperville, IL

This is the best bean casserole…everyone loves it!

23-oz. can pork and beans
15-oz. can butter beans
15-oz. can kidney beans
6 slices bacon, crisply cooked
    and crumbled
1 lb. ground beef, browned

2 t. mustard
1/2 c. onion, chopped
1/2 c. brown sugar, packed
3/4 c. catsup
1 t. salt
2 t. vinegar

Combine all ingredients well and spoon into a 2-quart bean pot or casserole dish. Bake, covered, at 350 degrees for one hour. Makes 8 to 10 servings.

Brightly colored linens, quilts and pottery add a festive feeling to a family picnic! Bring along a camera to record all the fun and lots of pillows for lounging.

Farmers' Market

Creamy Corn

Danielle Powers
Spearville, KS

This is my favorite side dish and I always have it on special holidays!

2 10-oz. pkgs. frozen corn
2 T. sugar
8-oz. pkg. cream cheese
1/4 c. butter
6 T. water

Place all ingredients in a slow cooker; cover. Cook on low for 4 hours, stirring occasionally. Makes 8 servings.

Old-Fashioned Pea Salad

Coli Harrington
Delaware, OH

Good with lunchtime sandwiches or served as a side with dinner.

10-oz. pkg. frozen peas, thawed
8-oz. can sliced water chestnuts,
    drained
1 c. celery, thinly sliced
1/2 c. green onions, sliced
1/4 c. mayonnaise
1/4 c. sour cream

Blend together peas, water chestnuts, celery and green onions. In a separate bowl, blend mayonnaise and sour cream; spoon over pea mixture and gently stir to coat. Serves 6.

Farmers' markets are brimming with beautiful flowers...violets, pansies, black-eyed Susans and daisies! Take advantage of those pretty posies and bring back the custom of May Day baskets. Fill a variety of baskets with sphagnum moss, layer in potting soil, then tuck in some favorite flowers. Very early on the first day of May, let the kids secretly set baskets on steps around the neighborhood!

Red Cabbage Toss

Linda Hosier
Huntingtown, MD

Just the right combination of color and crunch!

1/2 c. olive oil
2 T. sesame oil
1/4 c. rice wine vinegar
1 T. soy sauce
1 T. Dijon mustard
1/4 c. honey

1/4 t. pepper
1 T. toasted sesame seeds
1 lb. broccoli, chopped
1 c. red cabbage, sliced
1 c. raisins
1/2 c. chopped pecans

Combine oils, vinegar, soy sauce, mustard, honey, pepper and sesame seeds together; set aside. In a large serving bowl, place remaining ingredients. Pour dressing over salad ingredients; toss Makes 8 servings.

"Our summer band concerts were always held in a pretty park that was near a wonderful ice cream shop. The band played, fireflies came out, families brought picnics and children played...a favorite small town memory."

Jan Sofranko
Malta, IL

Farmers' Market

Maple Baked Beans

Kathleen Carlton
Hilton, NY

These always go fast...double the recipe for a large gathering.

1-lb. navy beans, rinsed
4 c. water
1 onion, sliced
1 T. margarine

1 c. maple syrup
1-1/2 t. salt
1 t. dry mustard
1 t. ginger

Bring beans to a boil in water. Reduce heat and simmer covered, for 2 hours. Drain beans, reserving 2 cups of liquid. Sauté onion in margarine until golden. Combine beans, onion and remaining ingredients in a 2-quart casserole dish. Bake, covered, at 350 degrees for 2 hours, adding reserved liquid if necessary; stir occasionally. Uncover and bake about 30 to 45 minutes or until all the water is absorbed and the top is slightly browned. Makes 4 to 6 servings.

All decked out for the Senior Prom!

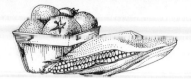

New England Corn Pudding

The Governor's Inn
Ludlow, VT

This is truly a wonderful, old-fashioned recipe!

8 T. all-purpose flour
1 t. salt
8 T. sugar
4 T. sweet, unsalted butter,
   melted

2 c. corn
4 eggs, beaten
1 qt. milk

Combine flour, salt, sugar and butter with corn. Mix together eggs and milk. Combine the milk and corn mixtures; pour into a 2-quart baking dish that has been coated with non-stick vegetable spray. Bake at 450 degrees for 45 minutes or until browned. Gently stir with a long-pronged fork, breaking the surface as little as possible 3 times during baking. Makes 8 servings.

Hometown champions!

Farmers' Market

Salmon Salad

Kathy Boswell
Virginia Beach, VA

Just right for a lunch with the girls!

1/4 c. French dressing
1/4 c. celery, diced
1/2 cucumber, peeled and diced
1/2 onion, finely chopped

7-3/4 oz. can salmon, drained
   and flaked
1 head lettuce

In a small bowl, combine all ingredients except lettuce; chill. Serve on lettuce leaves. Makes 3 to 4 servings.

Cucumbers in Sour Cream

Tammy Ebner
Harrisburg, PA

An old-fashioned salad recipe; remember this when your garden is overflowing with cucumbers!

1 c. sour cream
2 T. vinegar
4 T. sugar

1 cucumber, peeled and thinly
   sliced
salt and pepper to taste

Beat together sour cream, vinegar and sugar, fold in cucumbers; salt and pepper to taste. Makes 4 servings.

*"Our high school had a terrific basketball team!
In my senior year, we won eighteen games in
a row and went on to the State Championship
against our arch rival. No one has ever
forgotten the jump shot, from the center of the
floor. In the last seconds of the final game, we
won the championship by 3 points!"*

Donna Dye
London, OH

Apple Baked Sweet Potatoes

Linda Racher
Akron, OH

Tart apples and sweet brown sugar are perfect with sweet potatoes!

1 lb. tart apples, peeled and
    sliced
1-1/2 lb. sweet potatoes, peeled
    and sliced

1/4 c. brown sugar, packed
2 T. butter
1/2 c. apple cider

Alternate apples and potatoes in rows in a 1-1/2 quart baking dish coated with non-stick vegetable spray. Dot with brown sugar and butter. Pour apple cider over all. Bake, covered, at 375 degrees for one hour. Makes 8 servings.

*Create your own tablecloth and napkins that look as if they
have been handed down for years! Use fabric paint to
stencil a border of cheery red apples or cherries on
hemmed squares of white cotton or linen.*

Cheesy Broccoli & Rice

Jacque Caldwell
Spring, TX

A traditional side dish that's great for any family dinner.

10-3/4 oz. can cream of
    mushroom soup
10-3/4 oz. can cream of chicken
    soup
10-3/4 oz. can cream of celery
    soup

16-oz. jar pasteurized process
    cheese sauce
1 stick butter
16-oz. pkg. frozen, chopped
    broccoli
1 c. long-cooking rice, uncooked

Mix all ingredients together. Pour into a 13"x9" baking dish coated
with non-stick vegetable spray. Bake at 325 degrees for 35 to
40 minutes, stirring after 20 minutes. Makes 8 to 10 servings.

*There's nothing like a tire
swing for having fun!
Find a sturdy tree limb,
some heavy-duty rope
and a cast-off tire...an
instant hit with all the
neighborhood kids.*

Carrot Salad

Beth Eckenstine
Linden, PA

My grandmother created this recipe. I think it's a delicious and different way of serving carrots.

1 lb. carrots, diced	1/2 c. sugar
1 egg, hard boiled and chopped	1 T. all-purpose flour
1 T. celery, chopped	1/8 t. salt
1 T. onion, minced	1/2 t. dry mustard
1/4 c. vinegar	1 egg, beaten
1/4 c. water	1/2 c. milk

Add carrots to a large pot, cover with water and bring to a boil. Continue to boil until crisp-tender. Cool carrots and combine with egg, celery and onion. Set aside to prepare dressing. Blend together vinegar and water in a saucepan; bring to a boil. Stir together remaining ingredients and add to water and vinegar mixture. Simmer, stirring constantly, until thick. Set aside to cool and pour over carrots. Chill before serving. Serves 10 to 12.

"Our state fair in Washington was always a big treat for our family, but one year still stands out in my mind. When I was about 5 years old we went to the dairy booth and all the kids would get a free ice cream bar if they could milk the cow. When it was my turn, I pulled and squeezed, but there was no milk. Then, a dairy farmer showed me how to do it right and a tiny stream of milk came out! It didn't reach the bucket, but I still got my ice cream bar!"

Shirley Hudson
Spokane, WA

Farmers' Market

Scalloped Parsnips

*John Alexander
New Britain, CT*

An old family recipe.

4 c. parsnips, sliced
2-1/2 c. water
1 T. margarine
1 clove garlic, minced
1 T. all-purpose flour

1 c. milk
1/2 c. Swiss cheese, shredded
1/4 t. salt
1/8 t. pepper

In a medium saucepan, bring parsnips and water to a boil. Cover, reduce heat to a simmer and cook for 10 minutes or until tender; drain. Add margarine to a small pan and melt over medium heat; add garlic and sauté for one minute. Stir in flour and cook for one minute, stirring often. Slowly pour in milk and continue to cook over medium heat until mixture is thick. Add cheese and stir until melted. Mix together parsnips, salt and pepper, then add to cheese mixture. Continue to heat through for one minute. Makes 3 servings.

Ready to fly down the sidewalk trying to catch up with the other kids!

Gram's Cabbage Au Gratin

Shannon Wilson
Newark, OH

This is delicious! Gram used to make this for every holiday dinner.

4 c. cabbage, chopped and
   cooked
2 T. all-purpose flour
2 T. butter
1/2 t. salt

1/2 t. pepper
1 c. milk
2/3 c. Cheddar cheese, shredded
1/4 to 1/2 sleeve round, buttery
   crackers, crushed

Spread cabbage in a 13"x9" baking dish. In a saucepan, heat flour, butter, salt, pepper and milk; add cheese. Pour mixture over cabbage and sprinkle with cracker crumbs. Bake at 350 degrees for 30 minutes. Makes 6 to 8 servings.

Get family and friends together to enjoy some "child-like" fun! Play Kick-the-Can or Red Rover, enjoy a softball game, roast hot dogs, make S'mores and end the day with homemade ice cream!

Farmers' Market

Creamed Peas

Stephanie Moon
Nampa, ID

*My family loves creamed peas, and in my search for a good recipe,
I found a few, but none that quite matched what I wanted.
After some creativity, I came up with this recipe.*

2 c. frozen peas	2 T. butter
2/3 c. water	1/3 c. half-and-half
1 t. sugar	2 T. all-purpose flour
1/8 t. salt	1/2 T. sugar

In a saucepan, bring peas, water, sugar and salt to a boil; stir in
butter. In a small bowl, whisk together half-and-half, flour and sugar
until smooth and well blended; stir into peas. Cook and stir over
medium-high heat until thick and bubbly. Makes 4 servings.

*Glass milk bottles make
fun containers for
serving salad dressings!
Fill each bottle with
a different variety
of dressing and set
them around the table,
or place filled bottles in
a wire milk carrier...clever!*

Frosty Cranberry Salad

Ramona Higginbotham
Benicia, CA

I serve this salad in a large clear cut glass bowl...it's so beautiful!

2 3-oz. pkgs. raspberry gelatin
   mix
2 c. boiling water
8-oz. pkg. cream cheese,
   softened
2 T. mayonnaise-type salad
   dressing
8 oz. whipped topping

16-oz. can crushed pineapple,
   drained
16-oz. can whole berry
   cranberry sauce
1 tart apple, peeled, cored and
   chopped
1/2 c. chopped walnuts

Dissolve gelatin in water. Chill until partially set. In a medium bowl, beat cream cheese and salad dressing together until fluffy. Gradually beat in gelatin; fold in whipped topping. Add pineapple, cranberry sauce, apple and walnuts to gelatin mixture. Pour into a large bowl and refrigerate. Makes 12 servings.

Help the kids set up a summertime lemonade stand! Make a booth from old appliance boxes or push two card tables together...neighbors will line up to enjoy icy glasses of freshly-squeezed lemonade!

Frog Eye Salad

Tina Stidam
Delaware, OH

Don't let the name keep you from trying this recipe. This salad is so cool and refreshing, you'll love it!

1 c. sugar
2 T. all-purpose flour
1/2 t. salt
2 eggs, beaten
2 20-oz. cans crushed pineapple, 1-3/4 cup juice reserved
1 T. lemon juice

1 lb. box acini-de-pepe pasta, cooked
20-oz. can chunk pineapple, drained
3 11-oz. cans mandarin oranges, drained
1 c. marshmallows
16 oz. whipped topping

Cook sugar, flour, salt, eggs and pineapple juice over medium heat until thickened, stirring constantly. Add lemon juice; cool to room temperature. Add acini-de-pepe to sauce and refrigerate overnight. Add pineapple, oranges, marshmallows and whipped topping, mix gently. Makes 8 to 12 servings.

"I remember my girlfriends and I riding our bikes to town to get a cherry cola...it was great to be so carefree!"

Wendy Paffenroth
Pine Island, NY

Overnight Salad

Melinda Wilson
Centerville, TX

Since you make it the night before, this is great for busy families.

1 head lettuce, torn
3 to 4 stalks celery, finely chopped
4 to 5 green onions, finely chopped
8-oz. can sliced water chestnuts, drained

10-oz. pkg. frozen peas
1-1/2 c. mayonnaise-type salad dressing
1/2 c. sugar
1 c. Cheddar cheese, grated
1/2 c. bacon bits

Layer lettuce, celery, green onions, water chestnuts and peas in a bowl. Layer salad dressing on top of the layers and sprinkle with sugar. Cover and place in the refrigerator overnight. Before serving, add cheese and bacon; toss. Makes 8 to 10 servings.

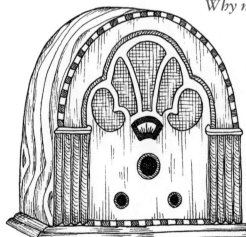

Why not choose an older neighbor or friend to "adopt" as a grandparent? This is great for your children, especially if their own grandparents live out of town. As a family you can do little service projects, washing windows, raking leaves, or weeding flower beds, that will be greatly appreciated.

Creamed Peas

Stephanie Moon
Nampa, ID

My family loves creamed peas, and in my search for a good recipe,
I found a few, but none that quite matched what I wanted.
After some creativity, I came up with this recipe.

2 c. frozen peas	2 T. butter
2/3 c. water	1/3 c. half-and-half
1 t. sugar	2 T. all-purpose flour
1/8 t. salt	1/2 T. sugar

In a saucepan, bring peas, water, sugar and salt to a boil; stir in
butter. In a small bowl, whisk together half-and-half, flour and sugar
until smooth and well blended; stir into peas. Cook and stir over
medium-high heat until thick and bubbly. Makes 4 servings.

Glass milk bottles make
fun containers for
serving salad dressings!
Fill each bottle with
a different variety
of dressing and set
them around the table,
or place filled bottles in
a wire milk carrier...clever!

Frosty Cranberry Salad

Ramona Higginbotham
Benicia, CA

I serve this salad in a large clear cut glass bowl...it's so beautiful!

2 3-oz. pkgs. raspberry gelatin
  mix
2 c. boiling water
8-oz. pkg. cream cheese,
  softened
2 T. mayonnaise-type salad
  dressing
8 oz. whipped topping

16-oz. can crushed pineapple,
  drained
16-oz. can whole berry
  cranberry sauce
1 tart apple, peeled, cored and
  chopped
1/2 c. chopped walnuts

Dissolve gelatin in water. Chill until partially set. In a medium bowl, beat cream cheese and salad dressing together until fluffy. Gradually beat in gelatin; fold in whipped topping. Add pineapple, cranberry sauce, apple and walnuts to gelatin mixture. Pour into a large bowl and refrigerate. Makes 12 servings.

Help the kids set up a summertime lemonade stand! Make a booth from old appliance boxes or push two card tables together...neighbors will line up to enjoy icy glasses of freshly-squeezed lemonade!

Farmers' Market

Fresh Tomato Salad

Carla Meredith
Belchertown, MA

This dish is at home with a more elegant meal or your basic backyard gathering!

4 yellow tomatoes, chopped
4 tomatoes, chopped
2 cucumbers, peeled and
  chopped
1 red onion, thinly sliced

3 to 4 sprigs fresh basil,
  chopped
salt and pepper to taste
1 c. vinaigrette dressing
Garnish: fresh basil

Combine all ingredients in a clear glass bowl; toss. Serve immediately at room temperature. Garnish with basil. Makes 6 to 8 servings.

Tortellini Salad

Mary Kitz
Waterville, OH

When looking for a dish to take to a potluck, this is the one I turn to.

9-oz. pkg. cheese and herb
  tortellini, cooked
6-oz. pkg. sliced pepperoni

14-oz. can artichoke hearts,
  quartered
12-oz. can black olives
1/4 to 1/2 c. Italian dressing

In a large serving bowl, combine tortellini, pepperoni, artichokes and black olives; toss with dressing. Chill for about 2 hours before serving. Makes 6 to 8 servings.

"I can remember walking with friends to the nearby ice cream shop. They had the best ice cream, but we always saved our allowances for the hamburgers because we liked them most of all!"

Gail Goudy
Walls, MS

Joe's Delight

Carolyn Waters
Crestview, FL

The aroma while cooking is so great, everyone will ask you what you are cooking. They also will ask "Who is Joe?"…my answer; "I don't know!"

1/2 lb. okra, chopped
1 onion, chopped
2 green peppers, chopped
2 T. oil
20-oz. can diced tomatoes, undrained

3 cubes chicken bouillon
1/2 lb. butter beans
1 clove garlic, chopped
1/8 t. salt
1/8 t. cayenne pepper
4 to 5 celery leaves

Sauté okra, onion and green peppers in oil until soft, but not brown. Mix in tomatoes, bouillon, beans, garlic, salt and cayenne pepper. Add celery leaves. Simmer for 2 hours, adding additional water if needed. Makes 8 servings.

Joining the Boy Scouts was a great way to make new friends.

Farmers' Market

Grannie Hobson's Louisiana Red Beans

Kristi Hobson
Grapeland, TX

This delicious recipe is a wonderful tribute to my Grannie Hobson.

1 lb. red beans
8-oz. ham hock
3 c. onion, chopped
1 c. green onion, chopped
2 cloves garlic, minced
1 green pepper, chopped
1/4 t. dried oregano
1/4 t. dried thyme

1 t. salt
1/2 t. pepper
1/2 c. fresh parsley, chopped
1/8 t. hot pepper sauce
1 T. Worcestershire sauce
1 lb. ham, chopped
2 t. oil

Wash beans by covering them with cold water; soak overnight. Place undrained beans and ham hock in a large stockpot adding just enough additional water to cover the beans; heat to boiling. Add all remaining ingredients, except ham and oil, and simmer for 2 hours. Brown ham in oil then, during last 30 minutes of cooking, add ham to stockpot. Makes 12 to 14 servings.

"Our neighborhood was quiet, but filled with many dear friends. In the winter we'd go sledding down a big hill, in late spring we'd go mushroom hunting and Mom would cook them for us. Summertime meant we enjoyed watermelon under the shade trees, then we'd wade in the creek trying to catch fish with our bare hands. Each fall we'd swing on large vines and jump into huge piles of leaves."

Michaela Topalov
Sidney, OH

Baked Sweet Onions

Barbara Hess
Boise, ID

I think these are absolutely the best!

4 sweet onions
4 T. butter, divided
salt and pepper to taste

8 T. fresh Parmesan cheese,
    grated and divided

Cut onions into quarters without cutting completely to the bottom. Place one onion on a 12"x12" piece of aluminum foil. Press one tablespoon butter into cuts in the onion; salt and pepper. Top with 2 tablespoons cheese. Crush aluminum foil around onion, but do not cover the top. Repeat with remaining onions. Place all onions in an 8"x8" baking pan. Bake at 400 degrees for one hour. Makes 4 to 8 servings.

Mushroom Casserole

Sylvia Fuller
Ashland, MA

I recently inherited Mom's handwritten recipe file and I'm so pleased to be able to share her recipe.

3 6-oz. cans mushrooms,
    drained
1-1/2 c. grated Parmesan cheese
salt and pepper to taste

1/2 t. garlic powder
1/2 stick butter
1/4 c. bread crumbs
2 T. parsley flakes

Mix together mushrooms, cheese, salt, pepper, garlic powder and butter. Pour into a buttered one-quart casserole dish. Top with bread crumbs and parsley flakes. Bake, covered, at 350 degrees for 15 minutes; uncover and bake an additional 15 minutes. Makes 6 servings.

To make your porch look especially patriotic,
tuck small American flags in your flowerpots!

Coconut Cake

Judy Kelly
St. Charles, MO

This cake needs to be made about 24 hours before serving. It has a wonderful flavor and a texture similar to a pound cake!

1 lb. butter
3 c. sugar, divided
2 c. all-purpose flour, divided
6 eggs
7 oz. flaked coconut

1 t. vanilla extract
1/2 c. water
1 t. coconut flavoring
Garnish: powdered sugar

Cream together butter and 2 cups sugar. Add one cup flour and mix well. Add eggs, one at a time, beating well after each. Add remaining flour, coconut and vanilla. Pour batter into a well greased Bundt® pan. Bake at 350 degrees for 50 minutes. Cool for 30 minutes and invert onto a serving platter. Simmer together remaining sugar, water and coconut flavoring for 5 to 10 minutes. Baste cake with glaze until all is absorbed. Before serving, dust lightly with powdered sugar. Makes 12 servings.

My very favorite birthday party was when all the neighborhood kids came. We even played Pin the Tail on the Donkey!

The Corner Bakery

Honey Bee Ice Cream

Lynda Tatman
Fresno, CA

Growing up, we all took turns cranking and sitting on the ice cream maker. After all these years, I can still hear the churning of the ice cream against the salt and ice.

1 c. honey
5 c. milk, divided
1/2 t. salt
4 eggs

12-oz. can evaporated milk
2 c. whipping cream
2-1/2 T. vanilla extract

Melt honey in saucepan with one cup of milk. Add salt to warm milk in pan. In blender, mix eggs, evaporated milk, honey mixture, cream and vanilla. Pour mixture into ice cream maker's freezer container and add remaining milk to fill line. Follow manufacturer's instructions for preparing ice cream. When ice cream is hard, drain water off and wrap in towel and let stand for one hour. Makes 24 servings.

"When I was young, sometimes in the summertime we'd have what we called an "ice cream supper". We would pile into the car and head to the ice cream parlor, then order banana splits, ice cream sundaes or parfaits...they really hit the spot on a hot summer night!"

Gentry Barrett
Holly Springs, NC

Old-Fashioned Apple Dumplings

Carole Zais
Rockford, IL

Tuck a pan of dumplings in a basket for a new neighbor or friend!

2 c. plus 3 T. all-purpose flour, divided
1 t. baking powder
1/2 t. salt
5 T. shortening
1/2 c. milk
2 to 3 t. butter

5 apples, peeled, cored and chopped
sugar to taste
cinnamon to taste
1/2 c. brown sugar, packed
1-1/2 c. boiling water
Garnish: whipped cream

Mix together 2 cups flour, baking powder, salt and shortening. Add just enough milk to moisten and form a ball. Spread on floured surface and roll dough ball with rolling pin to about 1/2-inch thick. Spread the top with butter. Lay apples across the dough. Sprinkle with sugar and cinnamon. Roll up jelly roll-style and seal ends. Cut in slices. Lay flat in a greased 8"x8" pan. Mix together brown sugar, remaining flour and boiling water. Stir constantly until thickened. Pour over apples. Bake at 350 degrees for 35 to 45 minutes. Top with whipped cream. Makes 6 to 8 dumplings.

Share the bounty of your apple tree! Make a batch of apple dumplings and place in a basket. A new neighbor, or favorite teacher would love receiving such a tasty surprise!

The Corner Bakery

Grandma's Bread Pudding

Karen Speten
Christine, ND

I think the sauce is what makes this bread pudding special.

4-1/2 c. bread, cubed	1/2 c. sugar
1/2 c. raisins or dried cranberries	1/2 c. brown sugar, packed
2 c. half-and-half	2 eggs, beaten
1/4 c. butter	1 t. vanilla extract
	1/2 t. nutmeg

In a large bowl, combine bread and raisins or cranberries; set aside. Combine half-and-half and butter in a saucepan and cook over medium heat until butter is melted. Pour over bread and let stand 10 minutes. Stir in sugar, brown sugar, eggs, vanilla and nutmeg. Spoon into a greased 1-1/2 quart casserole dish. Bake at 350 degrees for 40 to 50 minutes or until pudding is set in the center. Makes 8 servings.

Sauce:

1/2 c. butter	1/2 c. whipping cream
1/2 c. sugar	1 t. vanilla extract

Combine butter, sugar and whipping cream in a saucepan over medium heat and stir until mixture comes to a full boil and thickens, about 5 to 8 minutes. Stir in vanilla and spoon over warm bread pudding.

Life is to be fortified by many friendships.
To love and be loved is the greatest
happiness of existence.

-Sydney Smith

Caramel Crunch Apple Pie

DeNeane Deskins
Indian Harbor Beach, FL

Delicious, sweet apples with a crunchy walnut topping!

24 caramels
2 T. water
4 c. apples, peeled, cored and
   sliced
9-inch pie crust, unbaked

3/4 c. all-purpose flour
1/3 c. sugar
1/2 t. cinnamon
1/3 c. margarine
1/2 c. chopped walnuts

Melt caramels in water in heavy saucepan over low heat, stirring frequently until smooth. Spoon apples into pie crust; top with caramel sauce. Mix flour, sugar and cinnamon together; cut in margarine until mixture resembles coarse crumbs. Stir in walnuts; sprinkle over apples. Bake at 375 degrees for 40 to 45 minutes or until apples are tender. Makes 6 to 8 servings.

Store all the dry ingredients for your favorite pie recipe inside plastic zipping bags. Tuck bags inside a homespun-lined spongeware pie plate along with the recipe. Bring the corners of the homespun together and tie with strands of raffia...a delicious gift!

The Corner Bakery

Old-Fashioned Carrot Cake

Peggy Donnally
Toledo, OH

*Topped with yummy cream cheese frosting, you'll have a hard
time waiting for dessert to sample a slice!*

2 c. all-purpose flour
2 c. sugar
1-1/2 t. baking soda
2-1/2 t. cinnamon
1 T. pumpkin pie spice
1 c. oil

2-1/2 t. vanilla extract
3 eggs
1 c. raisins
1 c. chopped walnuts
3 c. carrots, grated

In a large bowl and by hand, mix together dry ingredients. Stir in
oil and vanilla. Add eggs. Fold in raisins, walnuts and carrots. Pour
mixture into 3 ungreased, 8" round cake pans. Bake at 350 degrees
for 25 to 30 minutes; cool before frosting. Makes 12 servings.

Frosting:

8-oz. pkg. cream cheese
1 stick margarine

1-1/2 t. vanilla extract
16-oz. pkg. powdered sugar

With electric mixer, beat cream cheese and margarine. Add vanilla. Stir
in powdered sugar and mix well. Frost cooled cake between each layer,
then sides and top.

*My childhood home was the home of a woman
with a genius for inventing daily life,
who found happiness in the
simplest of gestures.*

-Lora Fronty

Walnut-Oatmeal Cookies

Jo Ann

Have a plateful ready for an after school treat!

1/2 c. sugar
3/4 c. brown sugar, packed
1 egg
1-1/4 c. butter
1 t. vanilla extract
1-1/2 c. all-purpose flour
3/4 t. baking soda

3 c. quick-cooking oats,
  uncooked
1-1/4 t. cinnamon
1/3 t. nutmeg
2 c. chopped walnuts
1/2 c. chocolate chips

Mix sugars, egg, butter and vanilla together. Stir in dry ingredients, black walnuts and chocolate chips. Spoon by tablespoonfuls onto a baking sheet. Bake at 350 degrees for 10 minutes; cool. Makes 3 dozen.

Warm up a frosty winter's day by inviting friends over for an old-fashioned cookie exchange! It's a nice break from all the holiday hustle and bustle to relax with mugs of cocoa and chat with friends. Keep this get-together simple, friends only need to bring a dozen cookies...just enough for everyone to sample some of each.

The Corner Bakery

Boston Cream Cake

Sheri Vanderzee
Midland Park, NJ

Drizzled with rich hot fudge...perfect for chocolate lovers!

6 egg whites
1/2 c. applesauce
18-1/4 oz. pkg. yellow cake mix

1-oz. pkg. instant sugar-free
   vanilla pudding mix
1-1/2 c. milk
2/3 c. hot fudge topping, divided

With a mixer, beat egg whites for 30 seconds. Add applesauce and beat for an additional 10 seconds. Gradually add dry cake mix. Once entire cake mix is added, beat on high speed for 2 minutes. Divide and spread batter equally among 4 greased, 8" round pans. Bake at 350 degrees for 15 minutes or until a knife inserted in the center comes out clean. Cool in pans for 10 minutes. Remove from pans; cool completely on cooling racks. While cakes are baking and cooling, prepare filling. With mixer on the lowest speed, blend dry pudding mix and milk together for 2 minutes; refrigerate until cakes are completely cooled. To assemble cakes, place one cake layer on a cake plate or dinner plate. Spread half of the pudding mixture on the cake. Place second layer on top of pudding mixture. Spread 1/3 cup hot fudge topping on top of cake. Repeat for second cake. Keep refrigerated until ready to serve. Makes 16 servings.

*"When I was 14, my first job was at a local
5 & Dime. There were long aisles with oiled
floors, a soda machine with glass bottles and a
big candy counter. I had a special crate to stand
on so the customers could see me over the counter
and so I could reach the scale to weigh the candy."*

David Flory
Gooseberry Patch

Creme Puffs in a Pan

Jane Granger
Manteno, IL

Enjoy the sweet treat of creme puffs in this easy-to-make dessert.

1 c. water
1 stick margarine
1 c. all-purpose flour
4 eggs
8-oz. pkg. cream cheese

2 3-1/2 oz. pkgs. instant vanilla
    pudding mix
4 c. milk
8 oz. whipped topping
1/2 c. chocolate syrup

Bring water and margarine to a rapid boil. Remove from heat and add flour; beat with fork until mixture forms a ball. Place ball in a mixing bowl and add eggs, one at a time, beating well after each. Pour and spread mixture into a 15"x11" jelly roll pan. Bake at 400 degrees for 25 to 30 minutes; cool. Combine cream cheese, pudding mixes and milk. Beat until smooth and spread over pastry. When ready to serve, spread whipped topping on top of pudding mixture and drizzle chocolate syrup over pastry. Refrigerate before serving. Makes 12 to 14 servings.

"Each year on my grandmother's birthday, our family would always have a huge celebration. We'd all gather around the ice cream maker, waiting impatiently and eagerly anticipating a taste of homemade ice cream!"

Julie Hogan
Cornwall, VT

The Corner Bakery

Peanut Butter-Chocolate Bars

Corrine Lane
Marysville, OH

*This chewy cookie is just right for sending home with your nieces
and nephews. They'll love you even more!*

1/2 c. butter
1-1/2 c. graham cracker crumbs
14-oz. can sweetened condensed
  milk

1 c. peanut butter chips
12-oz. pkg semi-sweet chocolate
  chips

Melt butter in a 13"x9" baking dish in a 350 degree oven. When
melted, tilt baking dish to evenly coat bottom with butter. Sprinkle
graham cracker crumbs over butter, pressing lightly and evenly over
the bottom of the dish. Pour on sweetened condensed milk, top with
peanut butter chips then end with semi-sweet chocolate chips. Press
down on top layer so chips are in sweetened condensed milk. Bake at
350 degrees for 25 minutes or until top is golden. Cool and cut in bars.
Makes 2 to 3 dozen.

We always looked
forward to Sunday
afternoon rides in
Dad's new car! He
waxed and waxed it
until it gleamed!

Peachy Shortcake

Melanie Lowe
Dover, DE

Sweet peaches spooned on slices of warm gingerbread...wonderful!

14-1/2 oz. pkg. gingerbread mix
1 c. whipping cream
1/4 c. sugar

1 t. instant coffee granules
29-oz. can sliced peaches,
    drained

Bake gingerbread mix according to package directions. In chilled bowl, beat cream, sugar and coffee granules. Cut warm gingerbread into squares; split each square in half and top with whipped cream and peaches. Makes 9 servings.

Try some new ideas for decorating the tops of home-canned goodies! Country print fabric secured with raffia or jute, vintage handkerchiefs tied with ribbon, or squares of lightweight mesh screen held in place with thin wire.

The Corner Bakery

Blueberry Crumble

Vickie

Try this instead of traditional cobbler for a summertime dessert.

5 c. blueberries
9-inch graham cracker crust,
    unbaked
3/4 c. brown sugar, packed
3 T. all-purpose flour
1-1/2 t. vanilla extract

1/4 t. lemon zest
8 oz. sour cream
1/4 c. bread crumbs
1 T. sugar
1 T. margarine, melted

Spoon blueberries in crust; set aside. Blend together brown sugar, flour, vanilla, lemon zest and sour cream; spread evenly over blueberries. Mix together bread crumbs, sugar and margarine; sprinkle over sour cream mixture. Bake at 375 degrees for 40 minutes or until crumble is golden. Cool to warm before serving. Makes 8 servings.

"When my husband was a child, his grandfather would give him a nickel every Saturday. That night they would walk down to the general store together. He would buy an orange soda with his nickel and drink it while they sat on the steps and watched the men play horseshoes."

Darlene & Robert Koontz
Naples, FL

Coconut Cream Pie

Kimberly Davison
Nova Scotia, Canada

So creamy and a mile high!

1 c. flaked coconut
1 c. sugar, divided
3 c. milk
3 T. cornstarch
4 egg yolks, separated and
    divided

1/2 T. vanilla extract
1/8 t. salt
1-1/4 T. butter
9-inch pie crust, baked
Garnish: flaked coconut

In a large heavy saucepan, bring coconut, 1/2 cup sugar, milk, cornstarch, 3 egg yolks, vanilla, salt and butter to a boil. Stir constantly with a whisk until the mixture thickens. Pour into cooled pie crust. Blend together 4 egg whites and remaining sugar. Cover pie with meringue. Sprinkle with coconut. Bake at 350 degrees for 10 to 12 minutes or until top is golden. Cool before serving. Makes 6 servings.

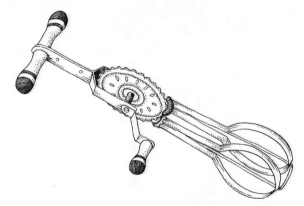

Come in the evening, come in the morning,
come when expected, come without warning;
thousands of welcomes you'll find here before you,
and the oftener you come, the more we'll adore you.

-Irish rhyme

The Corner Bakery

Peach Crinkle

Barb Bargdill
Gooseberry Patch

There's nothing like ice cream melting over warm peaches!

29-oz. can sliced peaches,
   drained
1 t. lemon zest
1-1/4 c. pie crust mix

3/4 c. brown sugar, packed
1/4 stick butter
Garnish: whipped topping or ice
   cream

Place peaches in an 8"x8" baking pan. Add lemon zest. Crumble pie crust mix and brown sugar together, mix well. Sprinkle brown sugar mixture evenly over peaches and dot with butter. Bake at 350 degrees for 45 minutes. Serve warm with whipped topping or ice cream. Makes 8 to 10 servings.

Remember going to the picture show on Main Street? Treat your kids to a Movie Marathon! Ask them to invite friends over and give them a stack of favorite classic videos! Serve lots of buttery popcorn, sodas, chocolate-covered raisins and they'll be set for an afternoon of old-fashioned fun!

Aunt Maggie's Apple Crisp

Mary Ott
St. Louis, MO

This is my favorite because I always use freshly picked apples. It just wouldn't be fall without this apple crisp!

4 c. apples, peeled, cored and diced
3/4 c. plus 1 T. all-purpose flour, divided
1/2 c. sugar
1 T. cinnamon

3/4 c. quick-cooking oats, uncooked
3/4 c. brown sugar, packed
1/4 t. baking soda
1/4 t. baking powder
1/8 t. salt
1/2 c. butter

Mix apples, one tablespoon flour, sugar and cinnamon together. Bake in an 8"x8" pan at 450 degrees for 15 minutes. Remove from oven and reduce heat to 350 degrees. Mix together remaining dry ingredients. Cut in butter with pastry blender until crumbly. Arrange topping on apples and bake for an additional 35 minutes. Serve warm. Makes 9 servings.

First haircut at the barber shop.

The Corner Bakery

Pecan Pie Bars

Linda Loar
McConnelsville, OH

Wonderful little pecan pie bars you can't stop eating! Great for a church social or holiday cookie exchange.

1-1/4 c. all-purpose flour	2 T. margarine, melted
1/2 c. plus 3 T. brown sugar, packed	1/2 c. corn syrup
1/2 c. margarine	1 t. vanilla extract
2 eggs, beaten	1/2 c. chopped pecans

Combine flour with 3 tablespoons brown sugar and add margarine until coarse crumbs form. Press into an 11"x7" pan. Bake at 375 degrees for 20 minutes. While crust is baking, combine eggs, remaining brown sugar, melted margarine, corn syrup and vanilla. Blend in pecans and pour mixture into crust. Bake for 15 to 20 minutes. Cool and cut into bars. Makes 18 to 24 bars.

"I remember as a kid cleaning my dad's barbershop on Saturday evenings after it closed. My mom and I would clean the bottles of hair tonic until they glistened. We'd sweep, mop and wax the floor until you could see yourself. For fun, I would sit in the barber chairs and make them go up and down and spin 'round and 'round. My dad always kept a stash of candy bars under the cash register that he would give the kids after their haircuts. That was the best part of cleaning...I would always get a candy bar before we came home!"

Vickie

Pumpkin Crisp

Peg Baker
La Rue, OH

This is a favorite fall recipe passed down to me by my Mom.

18-1/4 oz. pkg. yellow cake
   mix, divided
1-1/2 stick butter, divided
4 eggs, divided
29-oz. can pumpkin

1/2 c. brown sugar, packed
2/3 c. evaporated milk
2 t. pumpkin pie spice
1/2 c. sugar
1/4 c. chopped pecans

Mix together cake mix, reserving one cup cake mix for topping, one stick butter and one egg. Press into the bottom of a greased 13"x9" pan. Blend together pumpkin, remaining eggs, brown sugar, milk and pumpkin pie spice. Pour over cake mixture. In a medium bowl, combine reserved cake mix, sugar, remaining butter and pecans. Sprinkle over cake mixture. Bake at 350 degrees for 50 minutes. Makes 12 to 14 servings.

Don't be shy about entering your home-baked or home-canned goodies in the county fair. You never know when the bread & butter pickles your family can't get enough of, or the blueberry buckle your friends rave over will be a winner!

The Corner Bakery

Double-Berry Deep Dish Pie

Sherry Gordon
Arlington Heights, IL

*A terrific combination of raspberries and blueberries
in an old-fashioned cornmeal crust!*

1 c. cornmeal
1 c. plus 3 T. all-purpose flour,
   divided
3/4 c. plus 3 T. sugar, divided
2 t. baking powder
1/2 t. salt

3 T. butter
1/2 c. milk
2 c. blueberries
1-1/2 c. raspberries
1 t. lemon zest

Sift together cornmeal, one cup flour, 3 tablespoons sugar, baking powder and salt. Cut in butter until mixture is the consistency of small peas. Slowly pour in milk and gently stir until just combined. Shape dough into a ball, then divide ball in half. Using your hands, pat each half into a flat circle, wrap in plastic wrap and chill. On a lightly floured surface, roll out dough to a 12-inch circle. Place in a 9" deep dish pie pan. Roll out remaining dough for top crust and set aside. Gently toss together blueberries and raspberries with remaining flour, sugar and lemon zest. Spoon berry mixture into pie crust, add top crust and crimp edges to seal rim. Cut 3 or 4 steam vents in top crust. Bake at 350 degrees for 50 minutes to one hour or until golden. Let cool to warm before slicing. Makes 8 to 12 servings.

*At dusk, it's fun to gather
with friends for an informal
front porch party. Toss around
some cushions or spread out
a quilt, settle in and talk about
the day's happenings and how the
kids are doing. Relax, enjoy and keep
the refreshments simple...lemonade,
cookies or strawberry shortcake.*

Marvelous Macadamia Tarts

Nancy Ralston
Fresno, CA

You're sure to get "oohs" and "aahs" when you serve this!

1/2 c. margarine, softened
3-oz. pkg. cream cheese,
  softened
1 c. all-purpose flour
2 T. butter, melted
3/4 c. brown sugar, packed

1 egg
1-1/2 c. macadamia nuts,
  chopped
1 t. vanilla extract
Garnish: chocolate syrup

Blend together margarine and cream cheese. Mix in flour to form a soft dough. Chill at least one hour. Form dough into 30 golf ball-size balls. Place each ball into a mini muffin cup. With flour-dusted fingers, press into tart shapes. Blend together remaining ingredients; fill each tart shell. Bake at 350 degrees for 15 to 20 minutes. Cool; remove from pan. Drizzle chocolate syrup across tarts. Makes 30 tarts.

Take a spin on the traditional progressive dinner and have a progressive dessert party! Travel to each friend's house to sample her mile-high meringue pie, famous chocolate cake, or chewy raisin cookies. Don't forget to ask for the recipes, too!

The Corner Bakery

Blue Ribbon Banana Cake

LuCinda Jacobs
Gregory, MI

A handed-down and time-tested favorite.

1/2 c. shortening
1/4 c. plus 2 T. butter, softened
   and divided
2 c. sugar, divided
2 eggs
1 c. bananas, mashed
1 c. chopped pecans, divided
3/4 t. salt, divided

2 c. cake flour
1 t. baking soda
1 t. baking powder
2 t. vanilla extract, divided
1/2 c. sour milk
1/2 c. flaked coconut
2 T. all-purpose flour
1/2 c. half-and-half

Cream shortening, 1/4 cup butter, 1-1/2 cups sugar together; add eggs and bananas. Beat for 2 minutes. Stir in 1/2 cup pecans. Sift 1/2 teaspoon salt, cake flour, baking soda and baking powder together and add to banana mixture. Add one teaspoon vanilla and milk; beat 2 additional minutes. Divide batter equally between 2 greased and floured 9" cake pans. Sprinkle 1/4 cup coconut over batter and bake at 350 degrees for 25 to 30 minutes. Let cakes cool, then remove from pan after 10 minutes. Mix remaining sugar, flour, half-and-half and butter in a saucepan; cook until thick. Add remaining nuts, salt and vanilla; cool. Place first cake, coconut side down, on a serving platter; spread on filling. Place second layer, coconut side up, over first cake. Swirl on frosting leaving center of cake unfrosted so coconut can be seen. Makes 12 to 16 servings.

Snow White Frosting:

1 egg white
1/4 c. shortening
1/4 c. butter

1/4 t. almond extract
1/2 t. vanilla extract
2 c. powdered sugar

Cream together all ingredients except powdered sugar. Gradually add sugar, beating until fluffy.

Frosted Cashew Cookies

Jo Ann Smith
Kingfisher, OK

My favorite cookie...they just taste great!

1/2 c. butter, softened	3/4 t. baking powder
1 c. brown sugar, packed	1/4 t. salt
1 egg	3/4 t. baking soda
1/2 t. vanilla extract	1/3 c. sour cream
2 c. all-purpose flour	1-3/4 c. salted cashews, divided

Cream butter and brown sugar until fluffy. Beat in egg and vanilla. Add dry ingredients, alternating with sour cream; mix well. Fold in nuts, reserving some for the top of frosting. Bake at 400 degrees for 10 minutes on a greased baking sheet. Frost and top each cookie with a cashew. Makes 4 dozen cookies.

Frosting:

1/2 c. butter	1/4 t. vanilla extract
3 T. light cream	2 c. powdered sugar

Lightly brown butter in a pan. Remove from heat and add cream and vanilla. Gradually, stir in powdered sugar. Beat until thick.

"I remember going to the local drug store, sitting at the soda fountain and having a chocolate or cherry cola, but my favorite was the chocolate soda...yummy! Hamburgers were 5 cents each and after one basketball game we bought 50 to go!"

Karen & Jim Slack
Mt. Pleasant, TX

The Corner Bakery

Crushed Pineapple Cake

*Terri Lock
Waverly, MO*

Moist pineapple cake hidden under toasty coconut.

15-oz. can crushed pineapple,
   undrained
2 eggs
1/4 c. oil
2 c. all-purpose flour
2-1/4 c. sugar, divided
1 t. baking soda

1/2 t. salt
1/2 c. brown sugar, packed
1/2 c. flaked coconut
1/2 c. chopped pecans
1/2 c. evaporated milk
1 stick butter

Combine pineapple, eggs and oil; mix well and set aside. Sift together flour, 1-1/2 cups sugar, baking soda and salt; add to pineapple mixture. Mix well and pour into a greased and floured 13"x9" baking pan. Combine brown sugar, coconut and pecans; sprinkle over the top of cake. Bake at 350 degrees for one hour. Combine remaining sugar, evaporated milk and butter in a saucepan, bring to a boil; boil for one minute. Pour over hot cake. Serves 12 to 14.

*It feels so good
to have a friend on
whom you can depend.
A friend can help to mend
a heart, or boost you
toward a brand new start,
clown with carefree,
schoolgirl glee
and share a quiet
cup of tea.*

-Jan Miller

Chocolate-Pecan Pie

Jackie Crough
Salina, KS

Who doesn't like a big slice of chocolate pie?

3/4 c. chopped pecans
6-oz. pkg. semi-sweet chocolate
  chips
9-inch pie crust, unbaked
1/2 c. corn syrup

1/2 c. sugar
2 eggs
1/2 stick butter, melted and
  cooled
Garnish: whipped topping

Sprinkle pecans and chocolate chips evenly into pie crust. Blend corn syrup, sugar and eggs in medium bowl. Mix in butter. Pour mixture slowly and evenly into pie shell. Bake at 325 degrees for about one hour or until firm. Serve slightly warm or at room temperature. Garnish with whipped topping. Makes 8 servings.

A cookie basket will be much appreciated by a busy mom,
as well as the rest of her family! Securely wrap your favorite
unbaked cookie dough in plastic wrap, add the recipe,
jars of sprinkles, jimmies or colored sugar and even
a dozen baked cookies for her to enjoy right away.

The Corner Bakery

Old-Fashioned Peach Cobbler

Karen Moran
Navasota, TX

I enjoy this recipe most in the summertime with
a big scoop of vanilla ice cream.

3 c. plus 3 T. all-purpose flour,
   divided
1 t. salt
1 c. shortening
8 T. cold water
2 c. sugar

7 c. fresh peaches, peeled, pitted
   and sliced
1 c. water
1/2 t. almond extract
1/2 c. butter, divided

Combine 3 cups flour and salt; cut in half of shortening until mixture resembles coarse cornmeal. Cut in remaining shortening until mixture is consistency of small peas. Sprinkle cold water over mixture and stir gently with a fork until mixture holds together. Press dough into a smooth ball; divide in thirds. On a lightly floured board, roll out 1/3 of dough to 1/8-inch thickness, cut into small pieces about 3"x1" in size. Place on ungreased baking sheet and bake at 400 degrees for about 8 minutes or until lightly golden. Cover remaining dough with a clean cloth and set aside. To prepare filling, stir together sugar and remaining flour. Add peaches, water and extract; blend carefully. Roll out 1/3 of dough to 1/8-inch thickness, shaping to fit into bottom and up sides of a 3-quart baking dish. Spoon half of peach mixture into pastry; dot with half of the butter. Place cooked pastry strips over filling, then spoon remaining filling over cooked pastry; dot with remaining butter. Roll out remaining 1/3 of dough to 1/8-inch thickness, cut into 3/4-inch wide strips and arrange lattice fashion over filling. Trim edges; seal and flute. Bake at 375 degrees for 50 minutes to one hour. Makes 8 to 10 servings.

A soda shoppe treat...enjoy a pink or brown cow!
Just place a heaping scoop of vanilla ice cream
in a thick glass mug, then add some red pop
or root beer and enjoy!

Raspberry Fluff Pie

Susan Gress
Waterloo, IA

We cut each pie into quarters, so we can enjoy BIG slices!

1/2 c. orange juice
16-oz. pkg. marshmallows
2 c. whole raspberries, divided

2 T. sugar
2 c. whipping cream, whipped
2 9-inch pie crusts, baked

Combine orange juice and marshmallows in a double boiler until marshmallows are melted; chill until partially set. In a mixing bowl, combine one cup whole raspberries, sugar and whipping cream. Crush remaining raspberries, fold into mixture. Blend with marshmallow mixture and pour into pie crusts. Chill until set. Makes 12 servings.

"My favorite memory is of summertime block dances. Sections of Main Street would be roped off and hay bales scattered around for seating...the street lights and stars were our ceiling. When the boys came to ask us to dance, the excitement was almost too much to bear! When "Goodnight Sweetheart" was played, we'd pair off for the walk home dreaming of weddings, homes and lovely futures. It was a time I'll never forget."

-Sonia Schork
Lakeside, AZ

202

The Corner Bakery

Buttermilk Angel Food Cake

Leslie Cuff
Imperial Beach, CA

Such a wonderfully simple cake.

1 c. shortening
2 c. sugar
2 t. vanilla extract
4 eggs
3 c. all-purpose flour

1 t. baking powder
1 t. baking soda
1/4 t. salt
1 c. buttermilk

Mix shortening, sugar and vanilla together. Mix in eggs, one at a time, beating after each. Sift together all dry ingredients and add to shortening mixture. Add buttermilk and blend well. Grease and flour an angel food cake pan and pour in mixture. Bake at 350 degrees for 55 minutes. Makes 12 servings.

We always went to the soda shoppe after the double-feature movie...the chocolate sodas were the best!

Buttery Pound Cake

Cheryl Bierley
Miamisburg, OH

The sweet brown sugar glaze is just perfect with the apples!

1/2 c. plus 1/3 c. brown sugar,
   packed and divided
1/3 c. chopped pecans, toasted
1 t. cinnamon
1 t. nutmeg
3/4 c. plus 2 T. butter, softened
   and divided
1-1/2 c. sugar
3 eggs

2 t. vanilla extract, divided
3 c. all-purpose flour
1-1/2 t. baking powder
1-1/2 t. baking soda
1/2 t. salt
1-1/2 c. sour cream
1-1/2 c. apple, peeled, cored and
   thinly sliced
2 T. milk

Mix together 1/3 cup brown sugar, pecans, cinnamon and nutmeg; set aside. Cream 3/4 cup butter with sugar; add eggs and 1-1/2 teaspoons vanilla. In a separate bowl, sift flour with baking powder, baking soda and salt. Alternate adding sour cream and dry ingredients to butter mixture; beat well. Spoon half of the batter into a greased and floured Bundt® pan. Arrange apple slices over batter, then spoon half of the brown sugar mixture over apples; gently press in batter. Top with remaining batter, then sprinkle on remaining brown sugar mixture. Bake at 350 degrees for one hour to one hour and 10 minutes or until center tests done. Cool for 15 minutes, then gently loosen cake from pan. Let cool while preparing glaze. In small saucepan heat remaining butter over medium heat until it starts to brown. Remove from heat and stir in remaining brown sugar, milk and vanilla. Continue to stir until smooth and drizzle evenly over cake. Makes 16 servings.

Search flea markets, yard sales, or antique shops for unique biscuit and pickle jars and old-style bottles. They're just right to fill with sweet treats for friends, or to set on your counter filled with an after school snack!

The Corner Bakery

Mile-High Lemon Meringue Pie

Scott Harrington
Boston, MA

*My wife is in graduate school and whenever she has a big test
coming up I bake one of these to get her ready to study!*

1 c. sour cream
3 eggs, separated and divided
4-3/4 oz. pkg. lemon pudding
   mix
1-1/4 c. milk

1/3 c. frozen lemonade
   concentrate, thawed
9-inch pie crust, baked
1/4 t. cream of tartar
1/2 t. vanilla extract
6 T. sugar

Blend sour cream and egg yolks; stir in lemon pudding, milk and
lemonade. Pour in a double boiler and cook, stirring constantly. When
mixture begins to thicken, remove from heat and pour in pie crust.
Beat egg whites, cream of tartar and vanilla until soft peaks form.
Continue to beat, adding sugar, one tablespoon at a time, until egg
whites are stiff. Spread over pie filling, being sure meringue touches
edges of crust. Bake at 350 degrees for 12 to 15 minutes until golden.

*Have a "Swap-n-Shop" sale in your yard, garage
or basement! Friends and neighbors can bring gently-used
items they no longer need…clothes, furniture, books, or
glassware and swap with someone else for items they do want.*

Buttermilk Spice Cake

Zoe Bennett
Columbia, SC

Frost with your favorite icing or enjoy plain.

2 c. all-purpose flour
1/4 c. cornstarch
1 c. sugar
1 t. baking powder
3/4 t. baking soda
1 t. salt

3/4 t. ground cloves
3/4 t. cinnamon
3/4 c. shortening
1 c. buttermilk
3 eggs

Sift together flour, cornstarch, sugar, baking powder, baking soda, salt, cloves and cinnamon. Add shortening and buttermilk, beat until mixture is well blended. Add eggs, one at a time, and continue to beat one minute. Divide cake batter equally between 2, greased and floured 9" cake pans. Bake at 350 degrees for 30 minutes or until cakes test done. When cakes are cool, frost with your favorite icing if desired. Serves 8 to 10.

Flea markets and community yard sales turn up the best bargains! Search sale tables for nostalgic fabrics in crisp colors such as red, white, yellow, blue and green. Fabric can then easily be stitched into curtains, tablecloths or pillow cases!

The Corner Bakery

Chocolate-Banana Brownies

Elizabeth Resnick
Harrisburg, PA

If you like chocolate-covered bananas, try these brownies!

1/4 c. butter
1/4 c. bananas, mashed
1 c. sugar
2 eggs
1 t. vanilla extract

1/2 c. all-purpose flour
6 T. cocoa
1/4 t. baking powder
1/8 t. salt

In a large bowl, melt butter in microwave. Stir in bananas and sugar; add eggs and vanilla. Stir in dry ingredients until completely combined. Pour into a greased 9"x9" pan. Bake at 350 degrees for 30 to 35 minutes. Makes 16 brownies.

Enjoy an old-fashioned cake walk! Cut out pieces of construction paper in shoe-shapes, write a number on each and place them in a large circle. Each person chooses a "shoe" to stand on and music is played, sort of like musical chairs. Everyone walks around until the music stops and a number is drawn. Whoever is standing on that number wins a cake! Continue playing until all the cakes are gone.

Apple Fritters

Karen Walker
Stuart, VA

There's nothing like warm apple fritters with a glass of icy milk.

2 c. all-purpose flour
3/4 t. baking soda
1/2 t. salt
2 T. sugar
1/4 t. allspice
1/4 t. cinnamon
1/4 t. nutmeg

2 eggs, beaten
1-1/3 c. sour milk
2 T. shortening, melted
2 c. apples, peeled, cored and
    diced
oil
Garnish: powdered sugar

Sift together flour, baking soda, salt, sugar and spices. In a separate bowl, combine eggs, milk and shortening. Add wet ingredients to dry ingredients; beat until smooth. Fold in apples. Pour about 2 inches of oil into a deep fryer and heat to 350 degrees. Drop batter by spoonfuls into hot oil and cook to a golden brown turning once. Serve with sprinkles of powdered sugar. Makes 1-1/2 to 2 dozen.

The old fishing hole was good for more than just fishing! There was nothing like a jump in the water on a hot day.

The Corner Bakery

Gramma Brummet's Oat Cake

Barbara Briner
San Antonio, TX

A sweet-tasting, old-fashioned recipe.

1 c. long-cooking oats,
    uncooked
1-1/2 c. water
1/2 stick butter
1 c. sugar
1-3/4 c. brown sugar, packed
    and divided
2 eggs

1/3 c. all-purpose flour
1/2 t. salt
1/2 t. cinnamon
1 t. baking soda
2 T. butter, melted
1/4 c. evaporated milk
1-1/4 c. flaked coconut

Cook oats and water together; cool. In a mixing bowl, cream together butter, sugar and 3/4 cup brown sugar. Add eggs, one at a time, beating after each. In a separate bowl, sift together flour, salt, cinnamon and baking soda. Add dry ingredients alternately with oat mixture to butter mixture. Pour into a 9" pie pan and bake at 350 degrees for one hour. Mix together butter, evaporated milk, remaining brown sugar and coconut. Spread on cake and place under broiler until brown and bubbly. Serves 6 to 8.

"There's nothing like eating corn dogs, elephant ears and getting cotton candy all over your 3-year old face! The state fair was something I never wanted to miss! Where else could you see a life-size cow and calf made from butter? The fair was something that brought people together to celebrate summer."

Amy Blanchard
Ocean City, NJ

Malt Shoppe Pie

Becky Sykes
Gooseberry Patch

*The taste of this pie will take you back to the
days of old soda fountains!*

1-1/2 c. chocolate cookie crumbs
1/4 c. butter, melted
1 pt. vanilla ice cream, softened
1/2 c. malted milk balls, crushed
2 T. milk, divided

3 T. instant chocolate malted
   milk powder
3 T. marshmallow creme
1 c. whipping cream
Garnish: whipped cream and
   malted milk balls

Combine cookie crumbs and butter, press into a 9" pie pan. Place in freezer while preparing pie filling. Blend together ice cream, milk balls and one tablespoon of milk. Pour into pie crust and freeze one hour. Mix together malted milk powder, marshmallow creme and remaining milk. Fold in whipping cream and whip until peaks form. Spread over pie filling and freeze overnight. Garnish with whipped cream and malted milk balls. Serves 6.

Sock hops were such fun, why not recreate those memories by inviting friends over to listen to all that great 1950's music! Invite the girls to dress up in poodle skirts and saddle shoes, and the guys can wear tee-shirts and jeans. Teach the kids how to do The Twist, Hand-Jive and The Stroll.

The Corner Bakery

Peaches & Cream Pie

Natalie Tarr
Milton, WV

You'll enjoy this warm or cold!

3/4 c. self-rising flour
3-1/2 oz. pkg. instant vanilla
   pudding mix
3 T. butter, softened
1/2 c. milk
1 egg

15-1/4 oz. can sliced peaches,
   3 T. juice reserved
8-oz. pkg. cream cheese
1/2 c. plus 1 T. sugar, divided
1/2 T. cinnamon

Combine flour, pudding mix, butter, milk and egg; beat for 2 minutes. Pour into a 9" pie pan. Pour peaches into pie pan. Beat together cream cheese, 1/2 cup of sugar and peach juice; place on top of peaches. Combine remaining sugar and cinnamon; sprinkle on top of pie. Bake at 350 degrees for 35 minutes. Serves 6 to 8.

A pie eating contest is a tasty way for the kids to spend a sunny afternoon! Line up several individual pies along a table, have everyone keep their hands behind their backs, then dig in! Whoever finishes their pie first is the winner!

Strawberry Shortcake

Mary Murray
Gooseberry Patch

These are so easy to make, but no one will believe it!

3 c. strawberries, sliced
2 T. sugar
1 frozen puff pastry sheet,
   thawed

3 c. whipped topping
Garnish: powdered sugar

Toss strawberries with sugar; set aside. Unfold pastry and cut in 3 strips along fold marks, then cut each strip into 3 squares. Place one-inch apart on an ungreased baking sheet and bake at 400 degrees for 15 minutes or until golden. Set pastries aside until cool, then split each one in half. Spread the bottom layers with whipped topping, spoon on strawberry mixture and replace pastry tops. Sprinkle with powdered sugar if desired. Makes 9 servings.

Years ago, it was the custom to celebrate a strawberry regale each year, why not enjoy this simple and delicious pastime today? Serve all sorts of strawberry desserts...ice cream, shortcake, sliced strawberries and whipped cream, sherbet, or preserves spread on warm muffins...yum!

The Corner Bakery

Chewy Chocolate Clouds

Laura Fenneman
Lima, OH

I always take this recipe to cookie swaps...one batch is never enough!

1-1/4 c. butter, softened
2 c. sugar
2 eggs
2 t. vanilla extract

2 c. all-purpose flour
3/4 c. powdered cocoa
1 t. baking soda
1 c. chopped walnuts

Cream butter and sugar in a large bowl. Add eggs and vanilla, blend well. In a separate bowl, combine flour, cocoa and baking soda; blend into creamed mixture. Stir in nuts. Drop by teaspoonfuls onto ungreased baking sheet and bake at 350 degrees for 8 minutes. Do not overbake. Cookies will puff during baking and flatten upon cooling. Cool completely before icing. Makes 2 dozen.

Cloud Frosting:

3-1/2 oz. pkg. instant chocolate
    pudding mix
1/4 c. powdered sugar

1 c. cold milk
8 oz. whipped topping
Garnish: chopped nuts or cocoa

Combine pudding mix, powdered sugar and milk in bowl. Beat slowly with rotary beater or at lowest speed of an electric mixer until well blended. Let mixture stand 5 minutes before folding in whipped topping. Blend together. Ice cookies, and sprinkle with nuts or cocoa. Makes about 4 cups.

Happiness is like jam. You can't spread even a little
without getting some on yourself!

-Anonymous

Peanut Streusel Pie

Mary Hageny
Rhinelander, WI

This pie is so rich! Enjoy a slice with a tall glass of milk.

1/3 c. peanut butter
3/4 c. powdered sugar, sifted
9-inch pie crust, baked
1/3 c. all-purpose flour
1 c. sugar, divided
1/8 t. salt
2 c. milk

3 eggs, separated, beaten and
   divided
2 T. butter
2 T. vanilla extract
1/4 t. cream of tartar
1 T. cornstarch

In a bowl, combine peanut butter and powdered sugar. Place 3/4 of mixture in pie crust. In a saucepan, combine flour, 1/2 cup sugar, salt, milk, egg yolks, butter and vanilla. Stir on medium heat until thickened; set aside to cool. In a mixing bowl, combine egg whites, cream of tartar, cornstarch and remaining sugar; beat until shiny. Pour cooled flour mixture into pie crust. Top with egg white mixture; sprinkle with remaining peanut butter mixture. Brown in broiler and watch carefully. Makes 8 servings.

Fill several enamelware buckets with lots of ice and an assortment of treats...popsicles, fudge bars, juice pops, ice cream sandwiches and drumsticks, then invite the neighbors over for a backyard get-together!

The Corner Bakery

Sweet Angel Cupcakes

Roxanne Vilhauer
Jamestown, ND

Put several cupcakes in a lined basket with a note that reads,
"You're an angel!" A sweet "thank-you" for a friend.

18-1/4 oz. pkg. angel food cake
   mix
2 T. poppy seeds
1-1/2 t. almond extract, divided

1/2 c. sliced almonds, chopped
1-1/2 c. powdered sugar
1 T. plus 2 t. water

Prepare cake mix according to package directions, adding poppy
seeds and one teaspoon almond extract. Fill lined muffin cups with
batter about 2/3 full. Sprinkle batter with almonds, then bake at
350 degrees for 15 to 20 minutes or until tops are golden. Set aside
to cool completely. Combine powdered sugar, water and remaining
1/2 teaspoon almond extract, stirring until smooth. Drizzle icing over
cupcakes; allow to harden. Store in an airtight container. Makes
2-1/2 dozen cupcakes.

Keep a collection of colored sugars, jimmies, sprinkles and
edible glitter on hand to make your home-baked goodies special!
Sprinkle them on cupcakes, cookies and brownies…they'll
be the hit of the school bake sale!

Evelyn's Chocolate Torte

Norma Araceli Smith
Milwaukee, WI

This is always a requested dessert at family gatherings.

1 c. all-purpose flour
1 stick margarine
2 T. sugar
1/2 c. chopped walnuts
1/8 t. salt
11 oz. cream cheese

2/3 c. powdered sugar
12 oz. whipped topping, divided
2 3-1/2 oz. pkgs. instant
   chocolate pudding mix
2-1/4 c. cold milk
Garnish: chopped nuts

Mix flour, margarine, sugar, walnuts and salt together. Mix like a pie crust; when flaky, place into a greased and floured 13"x9" pan. Press around with fingers. Bake at 375 degrees for 10 to 15 minutes or until light brown; cool. In a large bowl, mix cream cheese, powdered sugar and 1/2 of whipped topping. Use an electric mixer and beat until creamy. Spread over cooled crust. In a separate bowl, mix pudding mixes with milk and beat for 2 minutes. Mixture should be thick. Spread over cream cheese filling. Top with other half of whipped topping and sprinkle with nuts. Refrigerate before serving. Makes 12 to 14 servings.

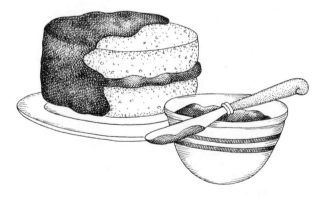

There's nothing like an invitation to share a cold winter afternoon with friends. It's fun to spend a lazy day playing board games and watching old movies. Take along a plate of warm cookies, crunchy peanut brittle or sweet fudge.

The Corner Bakery

White Texas Sheet Cake

Sandra Warren
Friendship, OH

A nice change from the chocolate version!

1 c. butter
1 c. water
2 c. all-purpose flour
2 c. sugar
2 eggs, beaten

1/2 c. sour cream
1 t. almond extract
1 t. salt
1 t. baking soda

In a large saucepan, bring butter and water to a boil. Remove from heat and stir in flour, sugar, eggs, sour cream, almond extract, salt, and baking soda until smooth. Pour into a greased 15"x10" baking pan. Bake at 375 degrees for 20 to 22 minutes or until cake is golden brown and tests done. Cool for 20 minutes. Spread frosting over cake. Serves 16 to 20.

Frosting:

1/2 c. butter
1/4 c. milk
4-1/2 c. powdered sugar

1/2 t. almond extract
1 c. chopped walnuts

In a saucepan, combine butter and milk; bring to a boil. Remove from heat and add sugar and almond extract; mix well. Stir in walnuts and spread over warm cake.

"Growing up, one of our favorite places to spend Saturday was the ice rink. As teens we were dropped off to spend the day ice skating, sipping hot chocolate and joining the circle of skaters to dance the Hokey-Pokey!"

Debra Severdia
Santa Rosa, CA

Nana's Blueberry Cake

Jane Hebert-Brazis
Saugus, MA

This cake always reminds me of afternoons with my grandmother teaching me to bake from scratch.

1/4 c. butter
1 c. sugar
1 egg, beaten
1-3/4 c. plus 2 t. all-purpose
    flour, divided
2 t. baking powder

1/4 t. salt
1/2 c. milk
1 t. vanilla extract
1 c. blueberries
Garnish: powdered sugar

In a large bowl, cream butter until soft, add sugar; mix together. Add egg and blend thoroughly. In a separate bowl, sift 1-3/4 cups flour, baking powder and salt together; add to creamed mixture, alternating with milk and vanilla, beat until smooth and light. Blend berries with remaining flour and fold into batter. Bake in a greased and floured 8"x8" pan at 350 degrees for 45 to 50 minutes. After cake cools, sift powdered sugar on top. Serves 6 to 8.

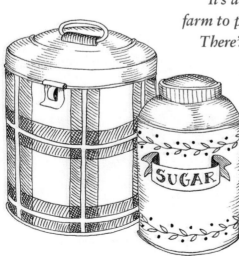

It's a lot of fun to go a berry farm to pick your own sweet berries! There's nothing like the taste of farm-fresh berries in a wonderful cake, cobbler or pie. Pack up the kids, fill up a thermos with frosty lemonade and have a great day in the country!

The Corner Bakery

Cherry-Pear Cobbler

Susan Kennedy
Delaware, OH

This is such a nice way to end a meal...sit, relax and chat with friends while enjoying this warm, sweet cobbler.

2 21-oz. cans cherry pie filling
3 pears, peeled, cored and
　　chopped
1-1/4 c. all-purpose flour
1/4 c. plus 1 T. sugar, divided

1-1/2 t. baking powder
1/4 t. salt
1 c. whipping cream
2 T. sliced almonds

Blend together cherry pie filling and pears in a 2-quart baking dish; bake at 400 degrees for 15 minutes. While fruit is baking, prepare batter by sifting together flour, 1/4 cup sugar, baking powder and salt in a large bowl. Gradually stir in cream with a fork, until mixture forms a thick, sticky batter. Remove baking dish from oven, drop batter by spoonfuls on top of fruit mixture. Sprinkle dough with remaining sugar, top with almonds. Bake 40 minutes longer or until biscuit topping is golden brown.

"As a young girl I would pick strawberries near our home and my grandmother made jam from them. I would stand near her as she stirred the berry mixture and just smell the air...the wonderful aroma of that jam is still with me today."

Sandy Benham
Sanborn, NY

Index

Index

Index

We've cooked up a whole collection of Gooseberry Patch® books!

Have a taste for more? Call us toll-free at
1-800-854-6673

We'll send you our latest catalog filled with snowmen, Santas, ornaments, candles, cookie cutters, gourmet goodies, salt-glazed pottery collectibles and MORE...including our best-selling cookbooks!

Phone us:
1·800·854·6673

Fax us:
1·740·363·7225

Visit our website:
gooseberrypatch.com

Send us your favorite recipe!

and the memory that makes it special for you!* If we select your recipe for a brand new **Gooseberry Patch** cookbook, your name will appear right along with it...and you'll receive a FREE copy of the book! Mail to:

Vickie & Jo Ann
Gooseberry Patch, Dept. BOOK
P.O. Box 190
Delaware, Ohio 43015

*Please include the number of servings and all other necessary information!

bakery · picnics · county fair · town square · picket fences · general store · ball park · barbershop · diner · pancake breakfasts · dry goods store · parades · soda shop · church suppers · festivals · 4-H Clubs · tag sales · farmers' market · bike shop